The People Value Proposition is an exceptional book. Dr. Stanley Harris provides a lifetime of lessons in humility, determination, leadership, and change management. Despite spending more than a decade as a physician CEO of a health system, I discovered many unique leadership insights in this book. The chapter on diversity and inclusion is especially perceptive and reflects Dr. Harris' remarkable career, which included more than a few encounters with racism and bigotry. His clear-sighted arguments in support of a more inclusive leadership style are fact-based and compelling without any hint of apology or regret.

His reflections on the lessons of COVID-19 and the murder of George Floyd are contemporary additions to his time-honored leadership adage of "see one, do one, teach one." His many examples of bringing leadership to life have benefited those of us who have had the good fortune of knowing him, and those who don't know him would benefit greatly from reading this superb book."

John M. Murphy, MD, FACP
President & Chief Executive Officer
Nuvance Health

The People Value Proposition is full of practical insights into what makes for good leadership shared through the life experience of a super talented and insightful physician leader. The reader is immediately captured by Dr. Harris's artful, deeply personal vignettes, making the book very real with applications to situations that all aspiring leaders can related to.

In addition, the relevance of diversity and inclusion today is manifest in the author's own history as an African American making it to executive ranks of modern American society. THANK YOU, Dr. Harris, for sharing this wonderful work that all of us attempting to lead can use to guide us as we chart our journeys forward . . ." See one, do one, teach one . . . LEAD!"

Minalkumar Patel, MD
Chief Executive Officer
Abacus Insights

i

Dr. Stanley E. Harris' book, *The People Value Proposition: See One, Do One, Teach One . . . LEAD*, offers aspiring and experienced leaders at all organizational levels both inspiration and counsel on the many challenges of being an effective leader. Through an in-depth personal reflection on his own leadership journey as a medical doctor and healthcare executive, Dr. Harris connects his own narrative and experiences to the essential practices that high-quality, high-impact leaders in any field or profession should aspire to.

This book offers a wealth of practical advice that is specific and actionable, all illustrated by personal stories and examples, to show how leaders can improve and deepen their own capacities and skills. It is an excellent volume for use in leadership development programs and in courses on leadership.

James P. Honan
Senior Lecturer on Education
Harvard Graduate School of Education

The People Value Proposition is much more than a guide to leadership, but rather a guide to being the best person you can be. Through stories and examples, Dr. Harris shares the kernels of wisdom he's gathered over the years – listen, lead by example, and don't forget the HUMOR (a handy mnemonic that sums it up). Two important sentences continue to resonate with me: "People are leaders' raison d'etre, their reason for being. Without people, a leader is just the one out front."

Daniel Halevy, MD FASN CPC
Vice President, Senior Medical Director, Healthfirst
Clinical Assistant Professor of Medicine, Robert Wood Johnson Medical School

Forget fire and brimstone, in a reasoned and scientific way, Stan Harris examines why we must value each other and why a people-focused approach to leadership is what we need in 2022 and beyond.

Alvin Patrick
CBS News Executive Producer

Stanley Harris wisely delves into the importance of engagement in *The People Value Proposition*. To establish an attentive, connected workforce, Harris asserts that team members must be valued and respected. I couldn't agree more. Our vision as a company is to inspire more human expression, connection, and celebration — for everyone. This means fostering a culture of inclusion where our team members feel respected, valued, and empowered. Harris provides inspiration and guidance for how companies can better galvanize and harness the very best of their workforce through intentional engagement.

Chris McCann
Chief Executive Officer
1-800-FLOWERS.COM, Inc.

Dr. Harris has been a leader in all phases of his life: student-athlete, physician, healthcare executive, and devoted family man. *The People Value Proposition* offers unique insight into the art of human relations – an important skill for anyone who wants to be a leader.

Dennis J. Murray, PhD
President Emeritus and Professor of Public Policy
Marist College

This book is a valuable resource that provides insight and perspective for new as well as established leaders. There is much to be gained from the wisdom and viewpoint of Dr. Stan Harris. A must read for those who want to apply the principles of "See One, Do One, Teach One . . . LEAD."

Alison Banks Moore
Vice President and Chief Diversity Officer
Horizon Blue Cross Blue Shield of New Jersey

THE PEOPLE VALUE PROPOSITION:

See One, Do One, Teach One . . . LEAD
A Physician's Journey to Leadership

Stanley E. Harris, MD, MA

Published by **American Association for Physician Leadership, Inc.**
PO Box 96503 | BMB 97493 | Washington, DC 20090-6503

Website: www.physicianleaders.org

AAPL books are available at special quantity discounts to use as premiums and sales promotions, or for use in corporate training programs. For more information, please write to Special Sales at journal@physicianleaders.org

This publication is designed to provide general information and is sold with the understanding that neither the author nor the publisher is engaged in rendering legal, accounting, ethical, or clinical advice. If legal or other expert advice is required, the services of a competent professional person should be sought.

13   8 7 6 5 4 3 2 1

Copyedited, typeset, indexed, and printed in the United States of America

PUBLISHER
Nancy Collins

EDITORIAL ASSISTANT
Jennifer Weiss

DESIGN & LAYOUT
Carter Publishing Studio

COVER ILLUSTRATION
David Bernardin

COPYEDITOR
Pat George

CONTENTS

*To my family and all who believed in me,
supported me, and mentored me, as well as
those whom I had the privilege to lead.*

ACKNOWLEDGMENTS

I offer my deepest gratitude to everyone who encouraged and stood by me when I had nothing, knew very little about anything, and had little hope of an education beyond high school. Fortunately, there were many who saw some value in me. From family who were willing to sacrifice and share whatever they had to the surrogate mothers, bosses, and friend at the tie factory in New York City, who knew I could be more than a shipping clerk.

Many thanks to the friend who had a similar vision and facilitated my entry into Howard University, an historically black university where I spent the first two years of my college education. It was at Howard that I first began to appreciate that vast cultural diversity in the world and realize the incredible array of intellectual and creative talents people of color possess. More important, I began to believe I could be more and do more than I had accomplished to date.

Doing more and becoming more is exactly what the instructors, mentors, and leaders of Marist College, the Albert Einstein College of Medicine, and the Montefiore Medical Center enabled me to do. They insured that I would succeed, be forever included in the process of effecting meaningful change, and have the opportunity promote the value in others. I am eternally grateful to them all.

I must also thank those who were gracious enough to take the time to critique my manuscript and provide insightful comments and perspectives that I hope are reflected in the quality of this book. They include: Michael McGarvey, MD, Dennis Murray, PhD, Sean D. Sammon, FMS, Robin Dillard Torres, MA, LMHC, Leslie Foxhall, and Amber Rabines, MSN, CNM, RN.

I am truly grateful for the step-by-step guidance, trust and support of Nancy Collins and the precise, insightful and patient feedback of my editor Patricia George.

Finally, to my wife Angela, without whom this book would have never been realized. For nearly 50 years, she has been my primary motivator, nurturer, writing instructor, and inhouse-editor.

ABOUT THE AUTHOR

Stanley Harris, MD, MA, is a physician executive with more than 30 years of experience in medical management operations and leadership development. He most recently served as senior medical director at Horizon Blue Cross Blue Shield of New Jersey, where he directed a team of physicians, nurses, and healthcare professionals who researched, developed, and coded medical policy that defined access to medically necessary care/benefits for 3.8 million subscribers. He also coordinated the meetings of the Physician Multispecialty Advisory Committee and the Professional Advisory Committee

Dr. Harris also served as the chairman of the Blue Cross Blue Shield Association National Medical Policy Panel, which consisted of medical directors representing more than 32 BCBS health plans across the United States. He also served on the Medical Advisory Committee of the Association.

He is a graduate of the Albert Einstein College of Medicine, where he served as an assistant professor of pediatrics and an assistant professor of epidemiology and social medicine and was a member of the Admissions Committee.

Dr. Harris completed his residency in pediatrics at the Montefiore Medical Center in the Bronx, New York, where he served as an attending physician and preceptor.

Dr. Harris also holds a master's degree in organizational communication and leadership from Marist College in Poughkeepsie, New York.

His first leadership position was as director of the Montefiore Comprehensive Health Care Center, an ambulatory care facility that served 15,000 families in the South Bronx.

He also was the assistant vice president for ambulatory care for the New York City Health & Hospital Corporation (NYC HHC), the largest municipal hospital system in the United States. He also served as medical director for alternative delivery systems for Empire Blue Cross Blue Shield; the service area covered the Eastern half of New York State from the Canadian border to the tip of Long Island.

A fellow of the NY Academy of Medicine, he has served as a member of its Institutional Review Board and the Pediatric Executive Council.

He also is a member of the Marist College Board of Trustees and is chairman of the Student Life Committee and of the Diversity and Inclusion Committee. Dr. Harris has been a member of the Health Services Advisory Committee of the Children's Aid Society of New York and a member of the New York City Infant Health Assessment Program.

Dr. Harris has spoken extensively on leadership and has delivered multiple presentations including the keynote on World Health Day at the United Nations.

Contact Dr. Harris at standrharris@gmail.com

INTRODUCTION

Do not read this book before considering the following questions:

- Do you believe the people you supervise, manage, direct, and lead are consistently performing at or above their optimal level?
- Do you believe you always communicate in a manner that engages, motivates, and inspires those with whom you are speaking?
- Do you consistently look for the value of each individual and let them know that you recognize and appreciate them?
- Do you believe that only those at the highest levels of an organizational hierarchy can lead?
- Do you seek the value in those you lead?

If you answered "yes" to these questions, you are unlikely to find this book to be of interest.

You are also unlikely to maximize the innate potential of those you lead.

If you did not answer all or some of the above questions in the affirmative, please read on!

THE PROPOSITION

We are experiencing a failure in leadership development, from corporations to courtrooms to communities. Respondents to a 2014 survey conducted by Deloitte of more than 2,500 organizations and human resources leaders around the world identified leadership development as their most urgent and important issue; 86% of those surveyed ranked the development of leaders as a critical concern. This is a shocking revelation when one considers we have hundreds of years of great leaders and hundreds of books about leadership to draw from.

This observation is further validated in "The Future of Leadership Development," published in the March-April 2019 edition of the *Harvard Business Review*. The authors state, "Several large-scale industry studies, along with our own in-depth interviews with clients, indicate that more than 50% of senior leaders believe that their talent development efforts don't adequately build critical skills and organizational capabilities. Few organizations are confident in and comfortable with the sustainability of their leadership teams.

The dedication to leadership development is one of the fundamental principles of the **People Value Proposition.**

The PROPOSITION

The People Value Proposition challenges both leaders and potential leaders to acknowledge and promote the value of every individual. This acknowledgment enables optimal utilization of resources, validates the principle that everyone matters, and initiates the creation of a perpetual cycle of leadership.

My goal is to enable you, whether you are an established or aspiring leader, to reassess who you are and how and why you lead. This is particularly relevant for those who were trained and work in the medical profession. Throughout my career as a physician, I have noted a reluctance by many to believe medical professionals can lead effectively. Yet, when I applied the principles of the People Value Proposition to my own life, the rewards were most gratifying.

In the chapters that follow, I share how I've learned to appreciate the importance of celebrating the value of those with whom I've lived, worked, learned, prayed, and played. Appreciating the value of others enabled me to succeed as a parent, physician, and leader. That appreciation has empowered others to emerge as leaders, enhance their functional capabilities, and deliver optimal results.

We must place a greater emphasis on developing those who have the potential to lead and improving leaders' capacity to facilitate that development, as expressed in the tenet "*See One, Do One, Teach One,*" which is an integral part of the **People Value Proposition.** I will discuss this further in the first chapter.

THE ESSENCE OF LEADERSHIP

To lead or to be a leader can be viewed in a simplistic context as one who goes first, finishes first, is considered the best in a particular field. A leader can also direct, guide, and motivate. A leader rallies a team to victory, inspiring action by capturing the hearts and minds of others. A leader may also define the vision, articulate the mission, or direct the formulation of a strategic plan for an organization.

Typically, the responsibilities, skillsets, and accountability of those in the executive suite far exceed those of people who supervise, manage, and direct various areas of an organization. It is important to realize that these skillsets and capabilities are acquired along the way to the top. Leaders must nurture and encourage the development of these essential skillsets in everyone who is responsible for executing the strategic plan and delivering results. This is especially true in the areas of interpersonal relationships, emotional intelligence, and communication.

Developing these skills comes from leadership opportunities, a commitment to continually learn, and a desire to succeed. As a medical director, I had contemplated pursuing a master's degree in business administration, public health, or healthcare administration, but could not convince myself to move forward. It was not until I decided to pursue a master's degree in organizational communication and leadership that my motivation was stimulated, and my resolve to learn more and become a better leader became a reality.

The perception of myself, what I was committed to and how I functioned, began to solidify. This educational journey provided a new, expanded intellectual infrastructure that supported a new sense of professional competence and confidence that was not part of my medical education and training. I began to reflect on where I began, how far I had come, and what I could have done better. This reflection led to deeper introspection and intensive assessment of those I have led and those who led me.

In addition, because I am trained in science and medicine, the knowledge I gained revealed intriguing insights into the enormous body of scientific literature that describes the way we think and act. The science identifies the specific parts of the brain and neurologic pathways that play a major role in executive decision-making and emotional reactions to stress, fear, and pleasure. This combined knowledge of science and leadership principles has become the basis for the way I think and lead.

Research on leadership frequently distinguishes between those who are leaders, as defined above, and those who are managers. One view is that a manager guides a team/department through processes, coaches, and develops each individual. A manager strives for optimal performance and better-than-expected results for the organization. Those results are not possible unless the manager, like a leader, is able to engage, inspire, and motivate others to effective action.

A leader provides the direction, but managers and supervisors chart the course and establish the objectives to accomplish the goals. The collective knowledge and experience of everyone executes the process or attains the objectives.

Dozens of people from every functional area step forward to lead. They may not have a title or be in charge officially, but they bring nuances of knowledge, compassion, inspiration, motivation, and experience that affect a team's ability to execute the defined objectives. These skills and attributes are most readily displayed when a leader is able to set the example. Leaders must consistently encourage the behaviors and support the actions that produce the desired results.

As the *Harvard Business Review* article indicated, the need to develop leaders at all levels is an urgent one for most organizations. The organization's culture must be structured to meet that need. Organizations must embed in their culture the premise that people are their most important resource. When people's value is recognized and allowed to evolve, their ability to create, adapt, and innovate can be infinite.

Throughout this book, my focus is those people who already have titles and are identified as leaders, as well as those who have the potential or the desire to lead. I alternate the use of feminine and masculine pronouns throughout the book to avoid being gender-specific, as I don't believe leadership qualities vary by gender. In Chapter 15, however, I specifically address the issue of the gender gap in leadership and pay.

The **People Value Proposition** applies to every organization regardless of size, how it defines its culture or how intensely it competes in the marketplace. I am confident that if you integrate the **People Value Proposition** into the way you lead, do business, and relate to people, your leadership skills will progress from ordinary to extraordinary.

REFERENCES

Angood P. *All Physicians Are Leaders: Reflections on Inspiring Change Together for Better Healthcare.* Washington, D.C. American Association for Physician Leadership; 2020.

Swartz J and Peister B. Human Capital Trends 2014. Deloitte Insights. 2014. https://www2.deloitte.com/us/en/insights/focus/human-capital-trends/2014/human-capital-trends-2014-survey-top-10-findings.html

Moldoveanu M and Narayandas D. The Future of Leadership Development. *Harvard Business Review.* March-April 2019. https://hbr.org/2019/03/the-future-of-leadership-development

CHAPTER 1

The Journey to Leadership

———

The potential to lead can be evident early in one's life.

In the beginning, there was high school and the incredibly complex, confusing, exciting, and sometimes depressing time called adolescence. By sophomore year, I was involved in many clubs and activities, and had joined the crew team, which was a truly enjoyable experience. It was exhilarating to be in the middle of the Hudson River, rowing in almost perfect synchronization with seven other guys to the rhythmic pounding of the coxswain on the side of the boat.

The enjoyment was short-lived, however. Halfway through the season, I quit the team after an unpleasant incident that had nothing to do with my rowing abilities.

After practice one day, I was riding with my teammates back into town. We came to a stop behind a line of cars at a red light, and in the car in front of us was a lovely little Black girl looking out of the back window. She flashed a big smile and waved — just a friendly wave to the car behind her.

Our driver's response was, "Turn around, you little Black bastard." He had forgotten I was sitting in the back seat of the car — the only Black crew team member. There was absolute silence, and all the other occupants avoided eye contact with me. When I was able to regain my composure, I asked to be let out at the next corner. I never returned to the crew team. Looking back, I deeply regret running away from an issue that I would encounter numerous times throughout my life. I now consider this as a failure to lead as a person of color in an all-white sport. Neither coaches nor teammates encouraged me to stay.

The episode served as an early lesson in assessing the boundaries of relationships with others. The fact that I was a member of a team, participated in club activities, or worked on school projects did not validate me as socially acceptable in some school activities or social events outside of school. Fortunately, this did not deter me from making friends and establishing relationships. When I was growing up, I never heard my mother use the word "hate" or see her harbor ill feelings toward anyone. I have subsequently realized that those who internalize hatred of another must live with it 24 hours a day and can be consumed by it. Thus, I was able to press on, choosing compassion over hatred, respect over rejection.

Throughout high school, I enjoyed positive relationships with classmates from diverse backgrounds and participated in a broad spectrum of school activities. These relationships apparently were positive and meaningful to my classmates and peers as well, as I was elected president of the junior class. How it happened was somewhat of a mystery to me. I was certainly not the smartest nor best-looking. I don't remember having a specific platform of witty slogans or appealing but ludicrous promises I could never have delivered. I do remember speaking directly to as many of my classmates as possible, offering a handshake and a smile, and pledging to do the best job possible as class president.

I proceeded through the year with great enthusiasm, basking in the glow that came with the honor and recognition of being a leader. My self-esteem took a nosedive after the Junior Prom. My date and I had not been invited to a single after-party. Our walk home was quiet and sobering, reminding me that how people view you in one context of your life is not necessarily how they see you in other settings.

In my senior year, I was prepared to run for president of the Student Government Organization. However, the school administrators informed me that I was ineligible to run for any office because I had failed typing. I have yet to understand how typing is a measure of my academic or leadership capabilities, but I believed that racism may have been the primary reason I was not allowed to run for the position. I was allowed, however, to participate in Government Officials City Day. Student leaders were selected to spend the day with key leaders of our city government. I was Corporation Council (the lead lawyer for the city) for a day.

Back at school, things were looking up.

For example, I was elected co-captain of the varsity football team. Although I was certainly not the fastest, biggest, or strongest player, I played both defense and offense and always gave everything I had.

I had been a "red shirt freshman," meaning the coaches thought my playing skills were good enough to move me up to the varsity team. During the last game of the season, I actually got in the game as a defensive end and made a couple of tackles, so by my senior year, I had been around longer than most of my varsity teammates.

As team captain, I led the team in warm-up exercises before each practice and game. I also set the bar for how the game should be played. I gave all I had every minute, in every game, while constantly pushing my teammates to do the same. I tried to lead by example.

Unfortunately, we had a losing record my senior year — not the way I wanted to end my athletic career. Did I fail as a leader? Perhaps. But I learned that sometimes your best is not good enough. I also learned that good people with good intentions might not be sufficient to successfully execute the job they are in.

When the senior yearbook was published, I finally had an idea why I was elected president and football captain: I was voted "Most Respected." When I looked at the comments my classmates wrote to me, I saw one phrase was repeated many times: "To a Great Guy."

To me, these remarks confirmed that the way I treated them made a difference. They knew I valued them as individuals, regardless of who they were or what activities they enjoyed. Valuing and respecting all people became a major guiding principle of my life.

My years in college were quiescent in terms of leadership development. I was married with a lovely baby daughter, carrying a heavy load of science courses and working small part-time and summers jobs. There was little time for extracurricular activities or social life. After graduating from college, I began a short career as a high school biology teacher. During this time, I underwent further maturation and introspection and developed a new vision of the person I could be.

When the opportunity to become a physician presented itself, I was ready to accept the challenge. My medical education and training would become a critical foundation for my leadership development.

SEE ONE, DO ONE, TEACH ONE

At 2 a.m., the phone in the on-call room jarred me awake. It was the intern (the equivalent of a first-year resident today) to whom I had been assigned for my first clinical rotation, pediatrics. "Meet me in the ER in five minutes, we have an admission," he said. I sprang from the bed, splashed some water on my face, swished some mouth wash, grabbed my white jacket and stethoscope, and was off to the ER.

I was a second-year medical student who, after a year and a half of didactic emersion and an introduction on how to diagnose diseases and medical conditions, was now experiencing the real thing. I was to help real people get better. My heart was pounding and my brain was churning with a combination of exhilaration and fear.

Since the dawn of formal medical education, the primary objectives for those aspiring to be in the medical profession have been:

- To understand how the human body works.
- To use that knowledge along with available tools and technology to diagnose, treat, or cure whatever problems were identified.
- To do so with integrity, caring, and compassion, while doing as little harm as possible to the patient.

Teamwork is expected and essential, but little time is spent providing explicit guidelines on how to achieve it. Similarly, little time is spent discussing how to lead such a team as one progresses through the hierarchy of the medical profession: student, intern, resident, attending, department chief. I was not only entering a new profession but also a unique culture.

When we entered the ER, the intern and I were handed the admission papers for a five-month-old infant. The child had been running a fever for nearly five days. The child's mother indicated that she had taken her baby to a local clinic three days earlier, and the child had been diagnosed with a virus. The mother was sent home with Tylenol and instructions to keep the baby well hydrated and return if the baby did not improve. Over the next two days, the child's fever persisted. She grew increasingly irritable, with decreasing appetite and a weak cry. The mother decided to go to the ER rather than the clinic.

The initial assessment did not identify the source of the child's illness; therefore, the child was being admitted for a workup of a fever of unknown origin.

We took the child directly to the examination room on the children's ward. The intern and nurses knew that a diagnostic workup required urgency and precision. There was much to be done, including a spinal tap (inserting a needle into the base of the spine to extract some of the spinal fluid).

The intern performed a thorough examination on the child to ensure no signs or symptoms not already noted in the ER were present. The resident arrived and immediately took charge. The nurses had assembled the equipment and materials to perform all of the necessary procedures for the workup. The resident turned to the intern and me and said, *"See One, Do One, Teach One"* as he prepared to perform the spinal tap. It was the first time I heard the phrase that would be repeated throughout my training.

The resident was leading by example — not only in his explanation of what he was doing in each step of performing the spinal tap and his courtesy toward the nurse who had everything he needed when he needed it, but also in his acceptance of the responsibility of developing the next one who would lead and teach. He recognized the value of everyone in the room — another lesson carried with me throughout my career.

The spinal tap was completed successfully and the fluid was sent to the lab. The infant was exhausted and somewhat dehydrated, and we still had much to do. We needed to start an IV (intravenous infusion) to provide urgently needed fluids and nutrients and obtain blood cultures to look for infection in the blood. Finding and inserting a needle into a vein in such a small arm was no easy task. After two attempts, blood was extracted for cultures, the IV was connected, and a urine sample was collected.

Now, we needed to determine the next steps in the treatment of our patient. The three of us sat in a small room to discuss the case. The resident reviewed all that we knew about the patient to this point and asked us for our thoughts. Based on the history, physical exam, and data we had at that point, we agreed to start the patient on broad-spectrum antibiotics until we received more test results from the lab.

This first real clinical experience left me with several indelible impressions. Although we did not have any explicit lectures on leadership or teamwork during medical school, they are repeatedly demonstrated in the See One, Do One, Teach One concept. This concept establishes the necessity of gathering all available information related to the issue to be addressed, determining what else is needed, formulating an action plan, and assembling a team to execute it. The execution requires the recognition of the value and role of everyone involved. It is time to embrace the **People Value Proposition**.

QUIET LEADERSHIP

Throughout my professional career and all that led up to it, I have strived to demonstrate, as Mahatma (Mohandas) Gandhi so aptly phrased it, that "Quiet leadership is not an oxymoron." "Quiet" does not imply that one is incapable of speaking up or standing up for those they lead. Passion, perseverance, and commitment do not have to be synonymous with an aggressive, vociferous exclamation of one's ability to lead.

Nor should "quiet" be equated with ineffective or indecisive leadership. It means moving forward with collaboration rather than indignation, focused thinking rather than meaningless distractions, and the realization that no leader knows everything.

My medical education and training taught me that displaying compassion, caring, and genuine interest in those with whom I work and seek to lead is not a matter of being "nice," but rather developing mutual respect and trust and setting an example. In my role as a father, I am reminded of conversations at the dinner table with our youngest daughter.

By the time she had reached the fifth grade, she was quite comfortable raising any issue for discussion. She was confident she would not be ignored nor asked to be quiet. She trusted and respected me as a reliable source of information and guidance. This was the case when we had a candid discussion about athletic supports (jock straps) for boys. It began with her question, "What happens to boys' "private parts" when they are running?" It concluded with my producing a clean jock strap at the dinner table and explaining how private parts are protected. I have had the pleasure of watching her take this same patient, respectful approach with her own children when responding to their questions.

Thus, these factors are an integral part of my leadership style and make it easier to provide constructive feedback and guidance. They also provide a solid foundation for supporting individuals and facilitating the development of leaders at every level of an organization. They reflect the essence of the **People Value Proposition**.

CHAPTER 2

Organizational Culture

————

*It is more about what you experience
than what you read and hear.*

An organization can be as small as a family, church, or school, or
as large as a mega-global corporation. Regardless of the size of
an organization or the nature of its work, people are essential for
getting things done. People listen to the customer, identify their needs and
concerns, then engage the appropriate resource to meet their needs or to
resolve their problems. Compassion, patience, and caring are primal needs,
and most people appreciate when these needs are met with help from another
human being.

Every leader must appreciate the critical role people play in decision-making.
People determine who, what, when, where, why, and how an organization
delivers expected results. Although digital technology such as artificial intelligence (AI) has become an integral part of most organizations, organizations
must use AI as an augmentation, facilitator, and enhancer of human intelligence, not as a substitute. When a goal or expected result is not achieved,
the people are held accountable, not AI.

Leaders are held accountable for outcomes, both positive and negative. Thus,
prudent leaders invest the time and energy to ensure they have the right
people in the right place at the right time. They also take the time to communicate the direction and goals of the organization. Leaders must clearly
articulate how critical the people they lead are in fulfilling the organization's
goals and vision.

People's perspectives, values, needs, and passions matter. Their ability to
satisfy the customer determines the longevity of the relationship. The client
or customer's experience with an organization is relevant to any organization and directly reflects its culture and leadership.

Everyone wants to be respected and valued for what they do. A leader who appreciates and acknowledges the value of others establishes trust and engages and motivates them. An organization that does not establish a culture to nurture, develop, and utilize the intellectual insight, practical experience, and innovative thinking of its people is unlikely to achieve sustained, optimal performance. It has not embraced the **People Value Proposition**.

At an organization meeting of a former employer, I asked, "What is our corporate culture?" The CEO answered: "*It's the way we do business.*" I spent the rest of the day pondering the meaning of that statement within the context of what I had seen, heard, and experienced during my years with the organization. The CEO and other leaders had never articulated or demonstrated a single theme, commitment, or principle. I was certain that tangible and intangible attributes defined this culture, but I was unable to envision them. Core values and vision and mission statements were posted in corridors, on the official website, and in printed materials, but did everyone within the company truly understand, believe, and consistently practice them?

Did the response "*It's the way we do business*" imply "by any means necessary"? How could I convey this concept of culture to my team without a more precise definition? Undaunted in my quest, I asked colleagues at every level of the organization, "What is our corporate culture?"

To my consternation, each response was preceded by a pregnant pause followed by an answer that differed from all those that preceded it. Most responses seemed to reflect a personal experience or series of actions taken by managers, but none embodied a concept embraced by the majority of employees.

The culture of the medical profession is highly competitive at all levels, from medical students to department chairpersons. Who can be proclaimed the best and brightest? Who has the stamina to work incredible hours? Effective communication with team members, patients, and their relatives is rarely discussed in morning rounds or didactic sessions. Yet, you still are expected to learn, be proficient in performing procedures, make appropriate decisions, and teach others to do the same. The culture is not designed to develop leaders; leaders emerge.

As I reflected on how to articulate the way an organization does business, I recalled the first real leadership role of my professional career. A year and a half after completing my residency, I was a primary care pediatrician working in a multidiscipline community health center. Located in the South Bronx, the health center was part of the Montefiore Medical Center Ambulatory Care Network. Eighty employees served more than 15,000 families.

When the top leadership position unexpectedly became open, to my surprise, the senior administrative team encouraged me to apply. They saw something in me that I clearly had not envisioned in myself. I applied and got the job. I had no formal training in healthcare management or leadership. I wanted to lead, but did I have the knowledge and skills to succeed?

I immediately gained an enormous amount of respect, trust, and ultimately love for my seasoned administrative team. It wasn't long before I began to appreciate the value each brought to the program. I was also eternally grateful that they saw my potential and were willing to nurture and support my ascent into a leadership role. Using the **People Value Proposition** principles, we set about creating a new culture for the center.

Love your staff.

I had already developed a deep affection for all the members of the staff. I could see the genuine caring and compassion they had for every patient and family. Every day, we found something to smile, laugh, or joke about. Moreover, everyone was acutely aware of the many daily challenges our families faced and were willing to go above and beyond the standards of good healthcare to try to make a difference in their lives. They were not just our patients; they were people whose needs we endeavored to meet.

For example, the staff collected clothing for a family whose apartment had been ravaged by fire and ensured a single mother had access to a food supplement program. They could readily appreciate the daunting task a mother of three faced to be on time for an appointment knowing she had to get each child dressed in winter clothing and take two buses just to get to the health center. I looked forward to going to work each day because of the way the staff addressed these kinds of challenges. Being at work was like being with family.

When I became the director, I had to step back to see the big picture. I needed to understand who we were, what our purpose was, how we related to each other, and how we were viewed by the outside world. This latter point was critical because at the time, our facility was surrounded by other entities commonly referred to as "Medicaid Mills."

The majority of these store-front organizations existed to generate as much income as possible by providing excessive, unnecessary tests and services with little concern for continuity of care or facilitating access to more complex care when needed. We clearly needed to distinguish our center from those around us. I knew that having a bright, shiny new building was not an immediate possibility, so we would have to work from the inside out.

The first step was to create a culture that would make that distinction evident to anyone who came through the doors — *a culture that was not expressed through words on a wall, but rather one that staff believed and practiced.* We needed to identify what would make us a better healthcare delivery facility. We also needed to determine how to make the best use of the individual talent and resources we had.

After multiple meetings with staff in every department and functional area, my administrative staff and I identified several steps to help define a new culture — one that our patients would experience as genuine, compassionate, and caring. I knew we had the right people to grow such a culture. We just needed to reframe our perception of each other and to understand and appreciate the value each contributes. This, in turn, would be manifested in the way we served our patients.

Each step was designed to send a clear message that every member of the staff was valued, that each individual made a difference in how well we functioned, the quality of care we provided, and how we were perceived by the outside world. The following are some of the steps we implemented:

Our registered nurses (RNs) previously had been relegated to intake stations behind a desk while nurse's aides were in the exam rooms preparing patients. We clearly were not making the best use of our nurses' clinical training. To remedy this, we offered our nurses additional training in physical diagnosis and brought them into the exam room with patients. They were now able to take more thorough histories, do preliminary physicals related to a chief complaint, and, if necessary, set in motion a treatment plan after consulting with a physician — for example, provide immediate therapeutic intervention for an asthmatic patient. They also initiated patient and parent education.

The nurses helped our patients and families feel that all their questions and concerns would be addressed.

The nurse's aide position, which had no career path for advancement within the existing medical system, was converted to administrative assistant, which did have multiple levels for possible advancement.

As part of their professional development, physicians on staff were allotted time to attend grand rounds (presentations on medical topics) at the medical center. They also were encouraged to make attending rounds at the hospitals in our system.

We also sought physicians' input on the design and content of our medical records. Long before the introduction of electronic medical records, all patient records were kept on handwritten paper charts in manila folders. Keeping track of these charts was the recurring nightmare of our medical records department.

When we took the time to investigate the problem, we discovered the main culprits were the physicians. They would hoard the charts with the intention of finishing notes once the tsunami of patients receded. Hoarding charts was not only a great disservice to the medical records department and to their patients, but also to their colleagues who cared for their patients when they were absent.

The addition of the nurses to the direct care process and the creation of a two-exam-rooms per physician design gave the physicians more time to complete charts and went a long way to alleviate the problem of missing charts and inaccessible data. Patients were able to move from the waiting room to the exam room more quickly. Staff had more time to gather information, and patients knew we were truly focused on them.

Our physical facility was fairly small by today's standards, and so was our maintenance staff. It became everyone's responsibility to help keep our place of work presentable. It was our home for at least eight hours a day, and we wanted our guests (families) to feel comfortable and welcome. The majority of our staff saw the value in this and took it seriously. Thus, picking up a scrap of paper in a corridor, keeping exam rooms tidy, and monitoring the cleanliness of the restrooms became everyone's concern.

I held a monthly all-staff meeting; however, there were always personnel who were unable to attend or whose department had issues that were not fully addressed in the allotted time. To adhere to my belief that everyone is of value and that what they do matters, we delayed the center's opening by an hour once a month to enable every department or functional area to meet to discuss issues or ways to improve their operational efficiency. In turn, the results of these meetings were reported to the appropriate senior administrative leaders for response and resolution.

To further solidify a culture built on the **See One, Do One, Teach One** mantra and the **People Value Proposition**, we encouraged every member of the staff to continue to learn and improve upon their responsibilities as part of our healthcare team. One way we did this was by creating an annual Universal Training/Education Day. We closed the facility for the day, and everyone, including maintenance and lab personnel, engaged in a learning experience, usually within the Montefiore Medical Center System. This opportunity exposed all staff to the latest techniques, equipment, and clinical knowledge.

This cultural transformation did not happen overnight; it evolved and developed over several years. The staff had a new sense of pride not only in the work we were doing but also in how we did it. We believed and lived a **People Value Culture**. However, I was still uncertain of how we were perceived by the outside world.

One day, as I was waiting outside our building for transportation to a meeting, two young ladies walked by pushing baby strollers. One said to the other, "Have you ever been in there? They are very nice, and it's clean too."

It was the affirmation I had been waiting for. The culture of respect that we had established internally spilled over to the way everyone who entered our facility was treated. It was not an acclamation about the quality care we provided, but it was a real example of the importance of respect. The respect enabled us to establish relationships with our patients built on trust. From there, we could deliver the best possible care.

It is the way we do business! The entire organization knew exactly what that meant.

Although our new culture included more meeting time, it was time well spent. Our operational efficiency and productivity improved significantly.

As a Maternal and Child Health, Section 330-funded program with a large Medicaid population, our profit margin was slim. However, it was sufficient to provide annual salary increments, purchase new lab and dental equipment, and retain most of our staff year over year. In addition, we were able to offer the staff some training and educational experiences.

The essence of an organizational culture is not what is written or proclaimed in an advertisement or posted on a wall. It is the embodiment of the daily energy and commitment the employees must exude. They have to do the best they can to support each other and to make everyone feel that they are the primary focus of attention when they need it. These principles apply to all settings that serve people.

REFERENCES

Chapman B. and Sisodia R. *Everybody Matters: The Extraordinary Power of Caring for Your People like Family*. New York: Penguin Random House; 2015.

Collins J. *Good to Great: Why Some Companies Make the Leap and Others Don't*. New York: Harper Collins; 2001.

Hasson G. *Mindfulness: Be Mindful. Live in the Moment*. New York: Fall River Press; 2013.

CHAPTER 3

Defining the Leader You Want to Become

If your actions inspire others to
Dream more,
Learn More,
Become More,
You are a leader.

—JOHN QUINCY ADAMS

Our vision of leadership is often shaped by the words conveyed in social and commercial media. Equally significant are the images portrayed in motion pictures, streaming services, and television, and, of course, the phrases and buzzwords (charismatic, dynamic, once in a generation) used to describe the leaders of various sports teams, titans of industry, or government officials. All of these characterizations of leaders may be valid references within a given context; however, were these individuals born leaders, or was their leadership developed through years of training and experience? I had an opportunity to think about this question during my early medical training.

I do not believe that leaders are born with the innate ability to lead. I do not believe they possess all of the skills and insights necessary to guide, inspire, and motivate others the moment they assume a position of leadership. Leaders are human beings who emerge from the combined impact of nature and nurture.

I use the term *nature* to refer to one's genetic (DNA) make-up: those 20,000 genes on 23 pairs of chromosomes that define our basic physical appearance, capabilities, and intellectual capacities — all of which can be modified, developed, or enhanced to some degree through dedicated training, education, and plastic surgery.

Nurture, I define as the collective, impressionable influence of parents or guardians, teachers, and mentors on an individual. Nurture also includes the impact of peer groups, entertainment outlets, social media, and online entertainment providers on how an individual experiences and sees the world.

Science has not been able to clearly determine when the influence of nature ends and that of nurture begins or vice versa. During my medical training, I enrolled in an elective course in child psychology and early childhood development that provided some interesting insights into the nature versus nurture question. Part of the program involved spending a day or two in two distinctly different daycare settings observing all aspects of the children's day.

The first daycare was in an affluent community in Westchester, N.Y. Many of the children were dropped off and picked up by nannies or stay-at-home moms. Two distinct episodes during these observations remain with me to this day.

One observation was of a group of three boys standing at a table upon which a wooden board had been placed. Each boy was given an appropriate-size hammer and some nails. Their task was to practice hammering nails into the board — an exercise intended to help develop hand-eye coordination and fine and gross motor control.

At one point, a fourth boy attempted to join the group. One boy had already given instructions to the other two as to where they should stand and clearly was the dominant member of the group. Although there was enough space at the table for another participant, he instructed the other boys to spread further apart, then turned to the fourth boy and said, "Can't you see there is no room for you here?"

Was this an example of an early innate ability to lead, nature versus nurture, both, or simply an example of bullying?

A second encounter in the same daycare program involved two girls playing in one corner of a sandbox. A boy with pail and shovel in hand tried to join the girls in their corner. After several requests for the boy to move to another spot, one girl picked up the boy's pail and shovel and carried them to a corner on the opposite side of the sandbox. She then stated very clearly, "This is your space; that is our space." Was this nature versus nurture, antisocial behavior, or an example of early conflict resolution skill?

The second site was a daycare program in the South Bronx. This memorable observation involved two children trying to play with the same toy. After tugging and yelling, one child pushed the other to the floor and took possession of the toy. When parents came to pick up the children, the child who had been pushed to the floor relayed the incident to his mother. Her immediate response was, "Did you hit him back? The next time somebody hits you, you better hit him back." Was this a lesson in survival of the fittest, a reflection of one's environmental influence, or a lack of nurturing?

Our perception of a leader can be shaped by many factors. Perhaps the most powerful influence on our impression of what a leader looks, sounds, or acts like is based on a personal encounter. Even then, a single encounter is rarely enough to appreciate the breadth and depth of one's leadership ability. The following elements serve as a frame of reference to define a leader:

Styles: transformational, transitional, authoritative, situational, autocratic

Transformational and transitional leaders are viewed as those who are capable of moving an organization from one operational, strategic, or cultural position to another. The actions taken may be driven by market demands, regulatory oversight, or social and cultural commitments.

The situational leader is able to adjust his style to the particular set of circumstances or employee personalities that will most effectively correct, rectify or resolve a critical issue.

The authoritative or autocratic leaders are often viewed as ones who seek their own counsel before that of others. These leaders tend to focus on exhibiting strength, control, and decisiveness and rarely show humility in their style of leadership.

Characteristics: charismatic, narcissistic, visionary, micro-manager, instructive, dominating, delegating, decisive, strategic thinker

Charismatic, visionary, and instructive are characteristics that tend to capture the hearts and minds of their followers.

The decisive and strategic thinking leaders readily command respect and trust when their actions prove to be beneficial to the organization and its employees.

The narcissistic, micro-manager, and dominating leaders tend to lead by instilling fear, with little appreciation of the value of others. They are most concerned with their own image and have little capacity for compassion or the development of others.

COMMON EXPECTATIONS

Leaders are expected to define the mission, inspire a vision, and exemplify the core values of an organization. We expect them to provide direction and maintain focus for an organization. The best leaders take every opportunity to communicate with the people on the front lines.

As the assistant vice president for ambulatory care in the New York City Health and Hospital Corporation (HHC), I led a team of more than a dozen college-educated facility liaisons/consultants who spent nearly every day in the field. Nevertheless, I still felt compelled to personally meet with the leaders of every facility that constituted the HHC Ambulatory Care Network.

At the time, it was the largest municipal hospital system in the United States, consisting of 11 acute care hospitals, multiple free-standing ambulatory care facilities, and skilled nursing and long-term care facilities. In addition, the system provided basic health services to families and individuals in homeless shelters.

I was responsible for the oversight of ambulatory care conducted in any of these facilities, including the emergency rooms at each of the 11 acute care hospitals, which generated five million visits a year. Each facility served communities with unique ethnic, religious, social, and cultural populations.

I wanted to learn firsthand what the leaders at each facility saw as their greatest challenges and how my team and I could best support and assist them in caring for the most underserved populations in New York City. Traveling throughout the city was a grueling but rewarding experience. The leader of ambulatory care was not just a name in the corporate office, but someone who genuinely cared and wanted to improve the delivery of care.

I recognize that a CEO or senior vice president does not have the time to sit around chit-chatting with thousands of employees. However, they do have time to engage one person at a time. The effective leader takes advantage of the opportunity to casually greet an employee in an elevator, a corridor, or in the cafeteria. This type of interaction promotes engagement and allows an employee to experience the actions of an effective leader and perhaps replicate them. Like the conductor of an orchestra, the leader must listen closely and pay attention to the work of each individual. The leader must draw out the best that each can produce and then blend them into a synchronized entity that consistently produces satisfying results.

Leaders are expected to be consistent and insist on adherence to the principles that frame the culture of an organization. They must be cognizant of their own actions and of those they lead to ensure the integrity and viability of culture.

PERCEPTIONS

If leaders believe an organization's culture is critical to defining what it is, then that culture must be embodied in and manifested by those they lead. This is best accomplished by the leaders' daily interactions with the people they lead. It is easy to claim, "we are the best," "we offer the best," or "we truly care about you." It is a challenge to deliver on those claims for every individual served by an organization, as well as those who work within it, which is why each interaction in the **People Value Proposition** matters.

CAPABILITIES

People are leaders' reason for being. Without people, a leader is just the one out front. It is possible to be a one-person band, but an orchestra is far more appealing.

Engaging people's hearts and minds is just the first step. Recognizing the value in each person and promoting sustained engagement are the real challenges. People want to be able to trust and believe in a leader. They also want a leader who believes in them.

The emotionally intelligent leader, with unquestioned ethical and moral standards, is a leader whom others will follow. Their desire to follow that leader will be influenced by the leader's willingness to learn, be part of rather than apart from an organization, as well as a desire to connect with and develop others.

Extensive research documents that the most respected leaders are those who use emotional intelligence. They are consistently described as leaders who:

- Share their knowledge and experience.
- Think and embrace core values to perform better.
- Enable others to complete a task by providing necessary resources and a clear explanation of its purpose.
- Understand a vision and help others appreciate it.
- Believe in the mission and commit to it.
- See the value in those they lead and appreciate the value in their colleagues.
- Acknowledge the value of a different perspective by taking the time to listen.

Emotionally intelligent leaders:

- Believe in the mission of an organization and understand the role of a leader.
- Believe a leader can make a difference.
- Have a clear perception of themselves and those they lead.
- Maintain an acute awareness of the economic, social, cultural, political, and regulatory environments that may impact objectives.
- Take the time to listen, understand, and empathize to better appreciate the challenges of others and the implications of decisions made.
- Manage and motivate not only through feedback, coaching, performance ratings, and bonuses, but also by finding the value in all individuals and helping them to understand the value of what they do.
- Communicate their expectations while still respecting the values, needs, and rights of others.

OTHER CAPABILITIES AND QUALITIES

Effective leaders have a range of other capabilities and qualities.

A *prudent* leader understands the importance of patience, persistence, and persuasion.

A *patient* leader can act with a sense of urgency when necessary. To be patient means to purposely take the time to see the big picture, incorporate the relevant variables, try to anticipate the potential consequences, then take the appropriate action.

A *persistent* leader has the courage and mental toughness to make decisions based on the best available information and stand by those decisions. A persistent leader also can see that an initial course of action is not going to achieve the desired results and may recalculate and perhaps consider the "road less traveled" to achieve an objective. A leader does not need to lower standards, compromise integrity, or abandon aspirations in order to exercise persistence.

A *persuasive* leader must believe in himself, establish strong values and adhere to meaningful principles. A persuasive leader needs to project and practice the behavior he expects of others.

A leader must be willing to challenge the status quo, to explore and learn about areas beyond her current knowledge base. A leader must empower and encourage others to do the same. A leader facilitates innovation and insists on accountability. Most importantly, a leader must continually reinforce with those she leads that they are valued and what they do matters.

When a leader is able to meet these parameters, understand the relevance of perspectives, and demonstrate these capabilities and qualities, she can deliver results that exceed expectations and sustain excellence. When a leader has incorporated these elements into a leadership style,

she is a leader— one who inspires and motivates others, one whom others will follow because they want to, not because they have to.

LEADERS AND THE PEOPLE VALUE PROPOSITION

Strong leaders follow the **People Value Proposition**. They create a perpetual cycle of leadership that enables others to lead and contribute in meaningful ways to an organization. Leaders who understand and become proponents of the People Value Proposition recognize it as an excellent way to strengthen an organization. The strength is measured in how effectively the teams of workers function in a competitive marketplace, how nimble they are in their ability to adapt to rapid changes, and how passionate they are about what they do.

Leaders also know that the viability, longevity, and sustained improvement of an organization are critical objectives they must accomplish. The critical elements needed to accomplish these objectives are the people and how well they understand the purpose, vision, and mission of an organization. These elements are guided through the People Value Proposition.

Leaders must recognize the value in each individual they lead. They must also communicate respect and develop trust. This communication is established through a genuine desire to connect, listen, and empathize. It also helps to create an opportunity for others to contribute and lead.

Finally, leaders should appreciate the importance of humor and how it can enable them to listen, connect and respect others.

REFERENCES

Bass BM. *Leadership and Performance Beyond Expectations.* New York: Free Press; 1985.

Druskat VU, Sala F, and Mount G. *Linking Emotional Intelligence and Performance at Work: Current Research Evidence with Individuals and Groups.* Mahwah, New Jersey: Lawrence Erlbaum Associates; 2006.

Goleman D. *Emotional Intelligence: Why It Can Matter More Than IQ.* New York: Bantam; 1995.

Harvard Business Review. *Best of HBR on Emotionally Intelligent Leadership, 2nd Edition.* Boston: Harvard Business School Publishing Corporation; 2008.

Hughes M, Patterson LB, and Terrell JB. *Emotional Intelligence in Action: Training and Coaching Activities for Leaders and Managers.* San Francisco: Pfeiffer; 2005.

CHAPTER 4

HUMOR in Leadership

───

Humor: More than laughter . . . .

HUMOR is an acronym for remembering essential elements for building a strong leadership foundation. Each element offers an opportunity for connectivity with those you lead. The elements also enable a leader to acknowledge the value of others, facilitate the continued development of skill sets, and enable the most productive application of those skills.

Many of the great leaders in the corporate world, political and military arenas, as well as sports, don't exhibit all of the elements discussed in this chapter. This is particularly true of the first one: Humility. For some, this word suggests a lack of self-confidence, an inability to act or think decisively, or the absence of "command presence." However, in my experience and that of many of others who are not at the very top of an organization but are still expected to lead, humility is an asset rather than a deficit. It can convey wisdom rather than weakness. It prepares the framework for empathy and the establishment of respect. Thus, Humility is the leading element of the acronym HUMOR.

H — HUMILITY

Leaders who demonstrate humility recognize the value of others. They have the courage to acknowledge that they don't know everything and willingly seek and accept the counsel of others. Leaders who exhibit humility rather than hubris inspire loyalty and respect rather than demanding it. These leaders connect with most people in a genuine and focused manner. No one is considered beneath them or unworthy of a moment of their time.

Each moment is time well spent. Time solidifies the cohesiveness of a team. Cohesiveness signifies a recognition of the importance of each team member in ensuring sustained, productive excellence. Through humility, leaders are able to show, not tell others, that they are sensitive to what team members may be experiencing, willing to listen to what they have to say, and appreciate their contributions.

By demonstrating humility, a confident leader acknowledges mistakes, accepts accountability, and commits to correct what is wrong or to explore what can be better. Practicing humility should be viewed as a lifelong process, with no definitive beginning or end. To be humble is a reflection of self-confidence and inner strength. It acknowledges imperfection while continuing to strive for perfection.

U — UNITY

To provide a clear direction, a leader must effectively communicate why what is being done relates to where an organization is going (purpose) and what must be accomplished (goal) to get *there*. The communication must emphasize that achieving a goal is a dynamic process that may require agility and adaptability. Understanding the purpose determines the resources to be utilized and the course of action to be taken. Thus, the unification of purpose and goal enhances the probability of achieving desired results.

Achieving desired results also depends on the consistent and effective implementation of one's responsibilities. The ability to consistently produce a quality product establishes credibility. However, one should not be lulled into the misconception that what one did today is all that one needs to do to meet the challenges of tomorrow.

The purpose and goals of an organization may be influenced by multiple factors in a competitive marketplace. These factors include regulatory environment, mergers and acquisitions, and the impact of social media on consumer decision-making. These factors and many others, such as the availability of personnel with the necessary skill sets, may necessitate the expansion or contraction of purpose, process, and goals. In the presence of so many variables, the reassessing or redefining of purpose, process, and goals is essential in order to ensure that they remain aligned.

M — MODEL BEHAVIORS YOU EXPECT FROM OTHERS

Being a leader is about being a role model for others, about setting an example and leveraging the power of See One, Do One, Teach One. This requires acting with integrity, awareness of the needs of others, and a willingness to share your knowledge with others.

For example, by showing passion for what you do, how you do it, and why you do it, you convey to those you lead that what each does collectively defines the organization and the quality of its work. Showing pride in what you do requires discipline, consistency, and vigilance. The ability to alter or correct a course of action and be adaptable enough to facilitate change are important actions for a leader to model.

Be generous with your praise for a job well done. Do so not only by speaking directly to the individual, but also by giving credit to the individual when conversing with those outside of your area. Promptly address mistakes — your own or the mistakes of those you lead. Mistakes should be teachable moments that precipitate learning and facilitate innovation. Mistakes can be opportunities for reflection, reassessment, and redirection. Feedback in the form of constructive criticism and coaching is essential.

If a problem appears to be beyond your scope of expertise, don't hesitate to seek the input of a knowledgeable source. This may mean going beyond usual resources and support systems. It may require engaging in a collaborative effort and demonstrating a willingness to share the credit for the development of a viable solution.

When you act in such a manner, you are demonstrating both confidence and wisdom. It sends a message that you will do what it takes to get the best results. You also provide a concrete example of a culture that encourages learning and sharing to succeed.

O — OPEN TO THE PERSPECTIVES, IDEAS, AND RECOMMENDATIONS OF OTHERS

Rein in any narcissistic tendencies and enable your vision to go beyond the reflection in the mirror. History is riddled with accounts of those whose quest for power, self-absorption, and disregard of counsel resulted in the collapse of empires and near destruction of entire nations. Lead with an open mind, encouraging others to share their perspectives and ideas.

Having the courage to forge new pathways and explore novel ideas is admirable; however, achieving the desired goals or objectives always requires the input, support, and commitment of those you lead. To be the best, you need to attract and retain the best. Your charisma, communication skills, and command presence may be excellent incentives for the best to join your team. Once they are on board, other factors such as ethics, integrity, and clarity of directions and expectations become relevant to the longevity of the relationship.

Those on your team need to feel connected and valued for what they do and who they are. Allow them to be their best by suppressing your fear that your power will be diminished or your authority usurped by having strong, capable people around you.

You cannot identify the best if you don't take the time to look for them. You cannot utilize the best if you do not appreciate their strengths and capabilities. You cannot be the best if you do not understand the importance of helping your staff improve and advance their careers.

R — RESILIENT, RELENTLESS, AND RESPECTFUL

Resilience conveys strength and durability. Challenges and setbacks are viewed as opportunities for reflection, reassessment, and redirection. Under no circumstances should they signal a time for withdrawal or isolation.

Be relentless in your commitment to help others do better, be better, and feel better about who they are and what they do. Insist on their best effort and willingness to use knowledgeable resources to achieve quality results. Part of being successful is knowing when to ask for help and where is the best place to get it,

When you convey a genuine respect for others, you will receive respect in return. Respect is a foundation for trust. A trustworthy leader inspires loyal followers who are willing to go the extra mile to get things done.

Finally, take HUMOR literally. Find time to laugh at yourself and with those you lead.

REFERENCES

Cockrell L. *Creating Magic: 10 Common Leadership Strategies from a Life at Disney*. New York: Doubleday; 2008.

Dame J and Gedmin J. *Six Principles for Developing Humility as a Leader*. Boston: Harvard Business School Publishing; 2013.

Rothberg H. *The Perfect Mix: Everything I Learned About Leadership I Learned as a Bartender*. New York: Simon and Schuster; 2017.

CHAPTER 5

Emergent Leadership

———

The opportunity to lead is more often felt than seen
more often a necessity than a choice
more often a commitment than a directive

Too often, those who can make a difference are overlooked and their value unappreciated. An organizational culture should encourage everyone to think, grow, and contribute. To limit or obstruct others' opportunity to speak up and be engaged means valuable resources go untapped. Good ideas wither and die. The cultural richness and strength of the organization are diminished.

The essence of emergent leadership is that one does not need a title or to be in charge in order to lead. The following examples illustrate this point:

On February 14, 2018, 17 students and teachers at the Marjory Stoneman Douglas High School in Parkland, Florida, were victims of a mass shooting. In the days that followed, students from Parkland and all across the United States stepped forward to articulate their heart-wrenching concerns about gun violence in our nation's schools. They led the most intelligent, compassionate, and determined protest to say, "enough is enough."

Students organized mass rallies, testified before Congress, and met with President Donald Trump. They demonstrated unprecedented perseverance to be the agents of change. They clearly represent future leaders who appreciate the value of each individual, as well as trust and respect for each other. They gave a voice to an entire generation of young people who have largely been ignored but are ready to emerge.

Leaders can emerge at any time, in any setting — something frequently seen in the world of sports. I am reminded of the young man who played on a junior varsity basketball team. At halftime, the team was down 10 points as the coach gathered the players in the locker room. Furious about their lack of effective defense, he repeatedly admonished the team's best player to do a better job of defending against the other team's high-scorer.

The young junior varsity player noticed that the coach had not given any specific strategy or suggestions for a better defense. He was certainly not the best player on the team, but he was a good student of the game and took particular note of who was doing what and when.

As the team was about to take the floor for the second half, the young man pulled the star player aside and offered the following advice:

"The guy we need to stop has scored most of his shots from about 15 feet from the basket; he can only move to his right with the ball. So, start guarding him further out from the basket. When he makes a move to his right, I'll slip over to help block his pathway and force him to the left."

Although the team lost by two points, the players played a much better game in the second half. This young man not only emerged to lead by sharing his knowledge and insight, but also offered to step up and help manage the problem.

Emerging leaders are individuals who, when placed in a novel situation, step forward to offer knowledge, insight, experience, or a new perspective. They are motivated not by a desire for self-advancement but by an impulse to help in a moment of need.

Unlike opportunistic leadership, emergent leadership is not about taking advantage of circumstances or showing little concern for the consequences to others. Emergent leaders believe their knowledge, experience, and dedication may be valuable to their team and organization. They recognize the necessity to interject, share, or recommend a different approach or perspective. Of course, this requires an organizational culture that facilitates such leadership. The culture nurtures and encourages them to seize the moment to share their knowledge — to lead.

Emergent leadership is different than situational leadership, in which leaders adopt a style of leadership best suited to the task before them or most applicable to those they want to move to act. It is closely aligned with the leadership competency of adaptability.

In her book *Quiet*, Susan Cain notes that one-third of Americans are considered introverts and are undervalued. The fact someone does not want to be in the spotlight does not mean their value should not be recognized and utilized. This again underscores the importance of a culture that encourages everyone to take the opportunity to share what they have, to add value, to lead. Quiet, introverted individuals are equally capable of leading.

I have never thought of myself as an introvert, yet I have often been described as a soft-spoken, quiet, and even-tempered individual. Still, when the opportunity to apply for the chairmanship of the Blue Cross Blue Shield Association National Medical Policy Panel arose, I applied and was appointed chairman. The panel was composed of medical directors representing more than 30 Blue Cross Blue Shield plans across the United States and Puerto Rico. I emerged to lead because I thought my knowledge and experience in medical policy would be valuable to the panel.

For me, it was confirmation that I had gained the respect and trust of my colleagues. It also highlights the characteristics of the Blue Cross Blue Shield Association National Medical Policy Panel as an organizational culture that nurtures and provides opportunities for individuals to come forward and lead.

Organizations whose leaders acknowledge the value, trust, and respect of others encourage emergent leadership. Emergent leaders are more likely to become engaged, motivated to step forward, take action, and effect change. At the same time, leaders who are not afraid to seek the input of emergent leaders around them, to openly acknowledge their contribution, and do what is possible to make them better are more likely to be successful leaders.

Every idea expressed by an emergent leader may not result in a time or cost-saving innovation. It may not be compatible with a strategic direction; it may be beyond functional capabilities or a replica of something already explored. The opportunity to express it, however, keeps the creative and innovative juices of the entire organization flowing.

REFERENCES

Cain S. *Quiet: The Power of Introvert in a World That Can't Stop Talking*. New York: Random House; 2013.

Epstein D. Range: *Why Generalists Triumph in a Specialized World*. New York: Riverhead Books; 2019.

Jayawickrama S. Developing Managers and Leaders: Experiences and Lessons from International NGOs. Hauser Center-Harvard Humanitarian Initiative Special Report, John F. Kennedy School of Government; 2011.

McKay M. and Fanning P. *Self-Esteem*. Oakland, CA: New Harbinger Publications; 2000.

Sanborn M. *You Don't Need a Title to be a Leader: How Anyone, Anywhere Can Make a Positive Difference*. New York: Doubleday; 2006.

Scroggins C. *How to Lead When You're Not in Charge: Leveraging Influence When You Lack Authority*. Grand Rapids, MI: Zondervan-Harper Collins; 2017.

CHAPTER 6

The Good, The Bad, and The Ugly

_____

Every word you speak is rarely remembered
but what you do often leaves a lasting impression.

Leaders are under constant scrutiny, judged as much by what they do and how they act in informal settings as they are by what they say or do in their formal leadership roles. Being a parent is an example. Every parent wants to be viewed as the leader of this complex organization called the family. Several illustrations in my family come to mind.

My two oldest children had not yet reached adolescence when I was rushed from work to the emergency room for evaluation of a sudden onset of an illness, later diagnosed as mononucleosis. When my son was brought to the ER, his only comment was, "Are we still going to the movies?" During my stay in the hospital for a diagnostic workup, my older child was unable to gather the courage to visit me. In both cases, my children were responding to the realization that their parent/leader, who had always seemed strong, was, in fact, quite vulnerable, a mere mortal.

Both children were now parents and leading their own families. When my son was preparing to paint the nursery in his home, I teased him and said, "I didn't know you were a painter." He responded in a very sincere and earnest manner, "I know this is what you would do." On another occasion, as my daughter and I were chatting, she commented that she noticed that I always treat people with kindness and respect, citing my interactions with gas station attendants, repair workers, and store clerks.

Through these examples, I began to appreciate that my many long-winded speeches at the dinner table and didactic monologues in the car may have been less impactful than what they heard and observed. I was leading by example and initiating a perpetual cycle of leadership within my family.

I have tried not to become complacent, self-absorbed, or convinced that my way is the only way to get things done. I take the time to reflect on where I started, how far I have come, and what is yet to be accomplished. Through interactions with leaders throughout my career, I have gained valuable insight into the spectrum of the good, the bad, and the ugly of leaders' behaviors. They ranged from the subtle, subconscious nuances in interpersonal relationships to blatantly offensive actions. In retrospect, some experiences I originally thought were bad were important lessons that provided the building blocks for my perspectives on effective leadership.

The following reflections are based on experiences or observations of mentors, supervisors, or bosses and do not always exemplify the principles of See One, Do One, Teach One. Some are my own epiphanies.

Early in my career, my mentor called my office at 7:30 a.m. two or three times a week just to see if I was at my desk. Initially, I resented the calls. I saw them as a sign of distrust or a lack of confidence in my ability to be a responsible leader. Frankly, I thought it was a *bad* tactic.

However, I soon found myself arriving at work before nearly everyone else. I now realize that those calls conditioned me to set the example for those I wished to lead. Not only was I on time, I discovered that I was productive during the peace and quiet of the early morning; it was a great way to prepare for the day ahead. Most of my administrative team consistently arrived to work on time, if not early. I don't know if I can claim any credit for this behavior because they had been leaders long before I joined the team.

This same mentor told me that he always arrived at meetings at least 15 minutes ahead of the start time. He didn't suggest that I do the same but, I readily adopted the habit and have never regretted it. It was a *good* leadership strategy.

During one of our frequent one-on-one meetings, the same boss/mentor pointed out that I gesticulated a lot with my hands when speaking. In this context, I concluded that these hand movements were a manifestation of my nervousness. I have subsequently learned that the appropriate use of your hands when speaking can be an effective way of emphasizing a point or engaging an audience.

I frequently met with my mentor in his very small office, which was furnished with a desk, two chairs, a couple of file cabinets, and no ventilation. You can imagine my displeasure when I had to sit through meetings with my boss while he lit a cigar and puffed away. I summoned up the courage to tell him of my distaste for the habit, but my expressed concern appeared to fall upon deaf ears, and the practice continued unabated. Ironically, I was less concerned about the effects of second-hand smoke and more about the thought that I would have to go through the rest of the day with my clothes reeking of cigar smoke.

To this day, I consider the cigar-smoking in that circumstance to be inconsiderate and disrespectful. This was a leader for whom I had a tremendous amount of respect, who failed to embrace the People Value Proposition. This was the *ugly* side of leadership.

One of a leader's greatest assets is the ability to recognize the skills and knowledge of those they lead. Core values, vision, and a strategic plan mean nothing if members of the organization don't understand them, believe what they do matters, and know their leader depends on them to make it all a reality. I've been fortunate to have several leaders who exhibited these qualities.

Early in my career, I was able to appreciate the value of those who manage processes, execute objectives, and achieve goals. I consider this a definite *good*. My appreciation of the good qualities in others has enabled me to recognize some of my own shortcomings.

For example, sometimes I talk too much. Perhaps it is a subconscious effort to demonstrate that I am not stupid or, even worse, revealing that I am. Unfortunately, I only appreciate those lapses "when the paste is out of the tube."

New employees from other areas of the company come to my office to get an overview of what my department does. Once I begin talking, it's as if I go on auto pilot. I am quite embarrassed and realize I have been very discourteous when a colleague asks if I would like to know something about the new employee and what they will be doing in the company. Oops, "the paste is out."

Several years ago, I took my granddaughter, who was four at the time, to lunch. As we were about to enjoy our pizza, the topic of calories came up.

She asked, "what's a calorie?" Aha! A golden opportunity for grandpa to demonstrate his scientific knowledge. After pontificating for about a minute and a half, my very bright granddaughter said, "Grandpa, l think I got it."

I am also guilty of breaking eye contact during one-on-one conversations. At times it is so obvious that the person with whom I am speaking turns around to see who or what is behind them. I have worked hard to overcome this fault.

I share these vignettes to emphasize that the fine-tuning of one's leadership skills should never end, and true self-awareness is a work in progress. For example, I appreciate the challenges for leaders to see and be seen and to ensure the "right" hands are shaken. However, I don't appreciate the fact that leaders who are "working a room" at a large gathering offer generic comments with their handshakes as they look past me to someone else. One can never be certain which hands and unmet eyes belong to a future benefactor or a stalwart team member. The most effective leaders are guided by the People Value Proposition and know everyone is of value.

A common theme intrinsic to the **People Value Proposition** is that leaders can be warm and engaging. They should make a genuine effort to know and appreciate those they lead. These attributes do not make a leader any less effective or authoritative. So, the following may be a bit of a contradiction as I share an example of the "*bad.*"

This leader would call a staff meeting of direct reports and ask each team member to share two things about themselves or their family that others may not know. This could certainly be viewed as a way for the leader to quickly learn something about team members and for them to learn something about each other. The problem was that, in the end, no business-related topics were discussed. It appeared as if the leader's mind was always somewhere else and that we were merely going through the motions of having an obligatory meeting. Individual meetings with this leader were no better. One could arrive with a list of agenda items, proceed through the list, and leave with no substantive feedback or guidance. If there was no topic for which the leader could claim credit, there was little substantive discussion.

I later learned that this individual had no real interest in leading, only in climbing as high as possible up the corporate ladder. As one might expect, this individual's tenure with the organization was short-lived. Throughout my career, I have encountered individuals who measure self-worth by believing that all successes, great and small, were due to their stewardship.

Another example of leadership deficit is the leaders who are so insecure with their self-image as leaders that all things thought to be of significance must appear to have been conceived by, driven by, or completed by their direct control. They must demonstrate that they are in charge. They are the motivating force and inspiration for all that is deemed of value.

This point was illustrated when one of the leader's direct reports completed a project that was intended to be a positive educational piece from the organization to the provider network. It had taken months to compile and represented a collaboration of internal and external expertise. However, when it was ready for distribution, the leader indicated he was "glad to get this out of the way" and did not acknowledge the potential value of the work to the organization or the effort of those who completed it.

This leader ignored subordinates in a meeting simply because he had no interest in or control over what the employee was doing or had to say. When things went wrong, he was adept at assigning accountability to someone else. This illustrates an *ugly* aspect of leadership.

I had the pleasure of working with three women who were outstanding leaders. They each led large, successful organizations through intelligent, insightful, and decisive leadership. They were each supported by a staff that held them in high esteem and showed genuine respect and fierce loyalty. Why? Because these women believed in the people they led. Show, don't tell, the behaviors, commitment, and compassion you expect from others.

CHAPTER 7

Seek Value

———

When you embark on the quest to seek value,
begin with yourself.
When value is established, success will follow.

B efore seeking value in others, you must appreciate your own value. If you don't believe in your own value, then it is nearly impossible to convince others of *their* value.

Acting with purpose and seeing the value in your work allows you to lead with direction. Begin each day by reflecting on who you are and how you are going to relate to the world around you. Be aware of your self-worth not in terms of monetary appraisal or introspective assessment, although these are certainly relevant elements of self-awareness, but on what you need to accomplish and why, and what role you play in achieving the objective.

Viktor Frankl, a psychotherapist noted for his own form of logotherapy (a derivative of existential analysis), which evolved from his experiences in concentration camps and is chronicled in his book *Man's Search for Meaning*, describes how he found a purpose for living when everyone around him was dying.

Faced with the reality that his wife, father, mother, and brother have all died in the gas chambers, stripped of all possessions, subjected to unbearable hunger and cruelty, Frankl is thus consumed with the question, "What is the purpose of life?" He concludes that every individual must identify their own purpose — a sentiment Frankl believes is the essence of a quote by Nietzsche: "He who has a *why* to live for can bear almost any *how*."

Frankl's purpose became the autobiographical documentation of an incredible atrocity of his time. He was so committed to this purpose that he wanted the first edition of the book to be published anonymously. It was only the constant urging of friends that convinced him to allow his name to be added to the next edition.

One must be in constant search of the why/purpose for one's existence and one's actions. The understanding of the why frequently extends beyond one's self to others. When Frankl asked his patients who had contemplated suicide whey they did not go through with it, their concern for others was the most frequent reason. This reason enabled them to define the how to continue living. This offers some insight to why and how one leads.

In every interaction, ensure you have a clear perception of your role and what aspects of your character and personality you need to project. Be sensitive to the bias you may bring to a discussion. Allow your mind to be receptive to different points of view and to the insights of those who may be closer to an issue than you are. Avoid releasing the burdens you carry onto others when it is not appropriate for them to share the load.

If you are meticulous, consistent, and honest in your daily reflections, you are prepared to turn your attention to others. By engaging others within a culture where every level of leader takes the time to listen and makes the effort to understand the relevance of the function of each individual, you discover each person's value and create opportunities for everyone to contribute beyond their daily responsibilities.

You must strive to promote a culture committed to identifying the assets of each individual, as well as the collective individual impact each has as a member of the team. As a leader, you must appreciate each person's work and support the importance of their appreciating each other.

When you acknowledge and promote the value of an individual's contribution to the success of an organization, you validate the significance of the work they have done. You announce to everyone that you are proud of the work accomplished and pleased to give credit where it is due. Hopefully, your affirmation gives an individual a sense of pride and accomplishment in a job well done.

The leader I most respect exemplified these qualities. Within his first two weeks of assuming the position, he visited key personnel in each functional area of my department to learn who they were and what they did. Although some staff members were intimidated by these meetings at first, they quickly came to appreciate that this leader cared about them and wanted to be as supportive as possible.

From these visits, our new leader gained valuable insight into my staff's work and its importance to the success of the organization. From these meetings and the team's ongoing performance, he gained confidence that this department was functioning well. He was comfortable focusing on other areas in need of guidance.

He was a leader people were happy to follow. He knew their value and didn't hesitate to tell the rest of the organization about them. This is an example of leadership in action that can be applied in any setting or organization.

Align the pursuit of value with a performance assessment and management strategy.

To accurately assess the talent and value of those you lead, your organization should have a valid system in place that supports performance management. Although the effectiveness of a system may be limited by financial restraints, the variation in the workforce responsibilities, and the ability of the management and leadership team to set and assess performance and improvement measures, these guidelines apply in most strategies:

- Develop metrics that focus on process improvement as well as productivity results.
- Determine if the measures proposed will have a direct or indirect impact.
- Assess the employees to determine if they are the right fit for their job responsibilities.
- Assess employees' satisfaction with their jobs and the organization.
- Strive to gain an appreciation of employee career aspirations and the availability of a pathway for employees to achieve them.
- Develop the ability to provide constructive, timely feedback and coaching.
- Commit to providing opportunities for individual development and enhanced leadership skills.
- Ensure that the organizational culture considers each employee an important, functional part of the company, not just a replaceable appendage.
- Insist on clear, consistent communication across all levels of the organization.
- Adhere to the premise that leadership development at all levels of the organization is necessary to sustain performance excellence.

The ability to define, capture, and analyze data points relevant to these elements depends on the technological capabilities of each organization. Once the data are obtained, the organization can determine how to design the most effective approach to performance management. No single approach is suitable for every organization.

Improving performance and delivering a quality product or service depends on how well everyone works together. It also requires a clear understanding of what resources, personnel, and other services are necessary to complete the work. Consequently, finding the value in each employee requires a well-developed performance management strategy.

Managers and supervisors are critical players in the performance management strategy. They are closest to the individuals on the front lines. They are charged with improving processes and meeting productivity metrics, as well as guiding and developing each individual. The leader who seeks value must ensure that all levels of leadership are prepared and committed to this objective. The approach must be consistent, fair, and accurate to ensure full engagement.

REFERENCES

Canwell A and Stockton H. Leaders at All Levels: Close the Gap Between Hype and Readiness. Deloitte Insights. March 7, 2014.

Corporate Leadership Council. *Building the High-Performance Workplace: A Quantitative Analysis of the Effectiveness of Performance Management Strategies.* Washington, DC: Corporate Leadersehip Council; 2002.

Frankl VE. *Man's Search for Meaning.* Boston: Beacon Press; 2006.

Sinek S. *Start with Why: How Great Leaders Inspire Everyone to Take Action.* New York: Penguin Group; 2009.

CHAPTER 8

Engagement

————

Without connection, there is no communication
Without communication, there is no direction
Without direction, there is no progress

A 2021 Gallup research poll indicated that only 36% of employees are engaged in their work. This lack of engagement translates into billions of dollars in lost productivity, creativity, and employee satisfaction. Establishing and sustaining employee engagement remains a significant challenge for organizations.

To facilitate engagement, organizations must ensure employees know that they are both valued and respected, that there is an opportunity to share and pursue an interest, vision, or goal. Employees understand that the skills, knowledge, and experience they have can be an asset to the organization. They feel a sense of inclusion.

Engagement is a springboard to motivation. Once employees see the connection between purpose and goal, their motivation intensifies and fuels the desire to make dreams a reality. When asked what motivated her, 20-year-old tennis player Naomi Osaka, who defeated Serena Williams to become the champion of the 2018 US Open Tennis Tournament, replied, "For me, I just feel like I like to break history, or make history."

From motivation comes inspiration that leads to innovation.

In 1941, as George de Mestral was walking his dog in the woods, he wondered whether the burrs that clung to his pant legs and to the fur of his dog could be converted into something useful. As he studied the burdock seeds under a microscope, he noted the many small hooks that made the seed cling tightly to fabric and animal hair. He had an inspiration: Perhaps he could develop something that would hold things together.

Inspiration is an unrelenting idea or vision that drives an individual forward. In de Mestral's case, it took 14 years. In 1955, he obtained a patent for Velcro, which today is used in everything from medical equipment to shoes. It's an innovation born of an individual's engagement in the belief that he could create something that could be of value to others. A leader must be aware of innovative resources within his organization and be willing to engage them.

The importance of engagement of people and resources within an organization is highlighted in the movie "Hidden Figures," which details the mathematical wizardry of Katherine Johnson and the computer analytic skills of the talented group of African-American women who performed mathematical calculations and analyses for NASA during the early years of the space program. Once these women were included and recognized for their skill and capabilities, their impact was quickly realized. Their work contributed significantly to the successful launch and landing of the first manned flight in the US space program.

Their innovative work exemplifies the importance of seeking value in, listening to, and utilizing the untapped resources within the people around you. Engagement stimulates creative thinking and the potential for new perspectives or solutions that may inform new paths. Employee engagement does not diminish a leader's ability or responsibility to be the final decision maker. It does help to identify the skill sets, knowledge base, and passions of those on the team. It also enhances the leader's ability to be more precise in knowing what to ask, how to ask, and whom to ask when making critical decisions.

One reality TV show, "Undercover Boss," offers a unique insight into the value of leaders taking the time to experience what their employees do and encounter on a daily basis and how they overcome challenges to keep the business operating smoothly at the ground level.

In each episode, the CEO of a company, disguised as a new employee, engages with employees on the front lines. Invariably, the leader comes away with a new appreciation for the incredible dedication and commitment of employees to do the best job possible. The leader realizes that employees are the enablers of sustained excellence and the agents of change.

In nearly every case, the leader identifies at least one employee who clearly "gets it," the one who is already leading, who understands the core values, embraces the vision, and believes in the mission. The leader invites the employee to the office for a face-to-face meeting at which the leader reveals his or her true identity. The leader shares the value of the undercover experience, what was learned and observed, and, most important, expresses gratitude and appreciation for the value the employee brings to the organization.

The undercover experience also identifies the employees who are not the right people for a specific job and are doing more harm than good. These individuals have a negative impact on fellow employees and on the reputation of the business, and are challenging employees for managers. The ways the leaders resolve these issues are teachable moments for leaders and managers.

For example, in one episode, the leader, manager, and a difficult employee had a face-to-face meeting during which the employee remained defiant and unrepentant in his attitude and behavior. After a brief discussion about possible approaches to the problem, the leader left the decision up to the manager, who immediately terminated the employee.

The ability to see or think about things differently offers the prospect of innovation and change. Those who are given the opportunity to express these new perspectives become the leaders within an organization. They become the new cadre of leaders to enter the perpetual cycle of leadership and represent the vanguard of the **People Value Proposition.**

KEY ELEMENTS OF ENGAGEMENT

The key elements of engagement range from simplistic and inexpensive, such as a smile, to staying connected to people you don't even see. This challenge includes concerns of ensuring collaborative, efficient teamwork, sharing insights and knowledge between team members who are working miles apart. Active listening becomes a critical skill, along with effectively communicating in a manner that conveys clarity, respect, and confidence in those you want to be fully engaged.

The Power of a Smile

Our brains are equipped with special neurons (cells) that enable us to automatically mirror or respond in a like manner or behavior projected by another person. Consequently, the smile is the most inexpensive, easily executed, and most-appreciated form of engagement. A smile has been scientifically and practically proven to be an easy first step in engaging most people.

It has always been easier for me to smile rather than to walk around with a grim expression, even if I was struggling with stressful issues just beneath the surface. It was not until I was a mature adult with a medical degree that I was able to grasp how a smile can instantaneously evoke a positive reaction.

I had just come out of a convenience store on Main Street in my hometown. For some reason, I was smiling. Perhaps the smile was from a pleasant exchange with the clerk inside or something I saw in the headline of the newspaper. As I proceeded down the street, an older gentleman walking toward me said, "I like what you are wearing." I had on a jacket, slacks, and tie, nothing exceptional. As I glanced down at my clothing, he quickly said, with a smile, "Your smile."

From that day forward, I have purposely tried to be a positive neuronal mirror. I smile on elevators, in stores, and whenever I can make eye contact with someone. A warm handshake and sustained eye contact also facilitate effective communication. I hope that setting a positive example will encourage others to do the same.

While a smile is an overwhelmingly positive tool for engagement in my life, this may not be true for everyone in every setting. A smile at the beginning of an announcement regarding impending layoffs is neither empathetic nor engaging. In the world of political correctness, a smile may be viewed as flirtatious. A smile can be a first step, but certainly not a mandatory one, to establish meaningful engagement.

Active Listening

Listen not with the intent to answer but rather to discover the perspectives, passions, and insights of others. Listen to become engaged in meaningful communication. Listen not just for agreement or validation of a point of view but also to assess whether the other person understands your intended message. As you listen, be sensitive to nuances that signal a lack of clarity or understanding of expectations. A slightly furrowed brow, a muffled sigh, widening of the eyes, or tilting of a head are a few clues that your comments may not have been as clear as you thought.

Communication Style

When leaders communicate effectively, their message is clear, and the potential for employee engagement increases. Conversely, if a leader's message is unclear or overshadowed by negative nuances or intonations, the recipient will likely focus less on the message and more on how it was delivered.

My mother was a housekeeper at a local college. Quiet, unassuming, yet dignified, she always carried herself with pride. She was able to command respect from nearly everyone she met. Students appreciated her kindness and generosity — she often invited students to Sunday dinner followed by long relaxing conversations. She listened attentively and was never judgmental. Students were pleased to have someone with whom they could share feelings of stress, anger, or frustration. Her responses were supportive and encouraging.

I often sought her council and deeply appreciated the guidance she offered and the example she set for how to treat people. I am eternally grateful for her lessons in humility, integrity, and generosity. Engaging in intimate, supportive conversations is increasingly difficult in today's work environment. Many managers and leaders have not developed the skills to participate in these exchanges.

Connections

The challenges of engaging those you lead are significantly increased when your team members work different shifts, are based in different locations, work from home, or are on leave.

In the last years of my full-time employment, most of my team members worked from home. I was fortunate to have a team of colleagues who had been with me for many years, so there was little danger of them being out of sight and out of mind. Nevertheless, I scheduled quarterly meetings to not only update the team on important business-related issues, but also to catch up with them about their families and their lives outside work.

My team members each had unique skill sets and knowledge bases that they could share easily when they sat next to each other in the office. Because these meetings were teleconferences, I did worry about the extent to which the staff members were able to relate to and support each other.

To get a better understanding of what was happening with the team, I set up individual sessions with each team member. I was happy to hear their ideas about improving our operational efficiency and was glad to learn that they made earnest efforts to connect with one another via computer and phone. Despite their demanding workload, nearly everyone was enthusiastic about doing what they could to sustain the level of excellence the team had achieved.

These sessions also helped me identify interpersonal conflicts, often caused by a lack of mutual respect or unprofessional communications. I followed up on each of these issues by inviting the participants in the conflict into my office for a face-to-face meeting. I began by asking each person to express what they thought the conflict was about. Then, I reviewed what I saw as the legitimate concerns of each party and engaged them in a discussion about why certain behaviors, intonations, or actions could be viewed as disturbing to the other. I ended each session by emphasizing the importance of being an efficient, effective team, which meant respecting the value that each member contributes.

These individual sessions reaffirmed their level of professionalism, commitment, and willingness to share their knowledge and experience. The interactions also provided an opportunity to stimulate more creative thinking and strengthen the bonds of engagement.

REFERENCES

Adkins A. Majority of U.S. Employees Not Engaged Despite Gains in 2014. Gallup. January 28, 2015. https://news.gallup.com/poll/181289/majority-employees-not-engaged-despite-gains-2014.aspx.

Edubilla.com. George de Mestral—Famous Inventor. www.edubilla.com/inventor/george-de-mestral.

Iacoboni M. *Mirroring People: The Science of Empathy and How We Connect with Others*. New York: Picador; 2008.

Roberts W. *Leadership Secrets of Atilla the Hun*. New York: Warner Books; 1985.

CHAPTER 9

The Power of Empathy

———

A genuine effort to understand
A sincere expression of caring and
A clear intent to listen are appreciated

Empathy promotes understanding and sets a framework for effective feedback. A clear understanding of an individual's perspective establishes a baseline for meaningful coaching and an opportunity to unify purpose with goals. Empathy also helps to communicate to an individual that what he does is appreciated and is of value.

Empathy allows a leader to appreciate an issue, subject, or action from someone else's perspective. The leader does not need to share the individual's emotions, stress, or frustrations in order to understand their impact on the person. More importantly, empathy enables a leader to show compassion and take action to improve a difficult situation.

Leaders must keep in mind, however, that empathizing with someone does not mean agreeing with them. Thus, it may be necessary to find common ground that allows everyone to implement meaningful changes.

THE IMPORTANCE OF LISTENING

Listening is a portal to empathizing. When you fail to listen, you miss an opportunity to coach, to identify a need for direction, or to simply help someone to be better. You miss a chance to understand the value of those you lead or to improve the conditions in which they exist.

Lyndon Johnson provides an excellent example of listening, empathizing, and acting to improve the lives of others.

In her book *Leadership in Turbulent Times*, Doris Kearns Goodwin recounts a period in Lyndon Johnson's life when he took a year off from college to become the principal of a small Mexican-American school in Cotulla, Texas. Kearns-Goodwin states, "Empathy fired Lyndon's efforts at Cotulla."

Johnson understood that his students were poor, often hungry, and subject to prejudice. They had little to look forward to once they left the classroom. The school had no funding for extracurricular activities, so Johnson used his own money to purchase sports equipment and lobbied the school board to fund other activities.

His efforts extended far beyond the classroom. He taught grades 5-7 classes; coached debating, softball, and drama; and led the choir.

Johnson knew that being able to listen and empathize with these students was not enough. Nor was it enough to say that he cared. As a leader, he set the example of what needed to be done by committing his time, energy, and money to making a difference. Thus, when he pressed his students to work harder, they did so willingly. They knew their teacher/coach/leader was not asking them to do anything he had not already done. His students said, "He put us to work, but he was the kind of teacher you wanted to work for."

Johnson was a master at engaging others. He was relentless in his determination to connect with everyone he met. He could convey empathy and communicate in clear, convincing language that became the hallmark of his political career.

EXPERIENCE VERSUS OTHERS' PERSPECTIVE

While I was in college, during my summer job at Western Printing and Lithographing Co., I was finishing my first night on the 10:30 p.m. to 7 a.m. shift. I was trying to move an electric flatbed hand truck used to transport pallets of books and paper.

Unfortunately, I was working close to the time clock where folks were rushing to punch their timecards. I panicked and accidentally slammed the flatbed into the ankle of a woman trying to reach the time clock. She went down screaming in pain. The damage was severe enough that she had to be transported to the hospital for stitches in her ankle.

At that moment, I was devastated, and certain I would lose my job. More important, I could not get the vision of the woman crumpled in agony on the floor out of my mind. I needed to know who she was and the extent of the damage I had done.

When my fellow employees identified my victim, they didn't hesitate to tell me she was not a pleasant individual. It didn't matter. I was racked with guilt and needed to find out how she was doing. My foreman gave me her phone number and I dialed with palpable apprehension.

When she answered, I quickly identified myself as the idiot who tried to run over her at work and blurted out a plethora of apologies. When I had run out of breath, she quietly said, "It's okay, these things happen. I know you did not do it on purpose." She thanked me for calling and hung up. In this case, I believe she was able to empathize more with me more than I had with her. She listened to this young, frightened voice on the phone and cared enough to forgive me.

She was not the difficult person my colleagues had described. That experience taught me to listen to others, to take their opinions under advisement, but to depend on my own personal interactions before reaching a final judgment.

DIGGING FOR THE DETAILS

The lesson served me well in my role as medical director for a large health maintenance organization (HMO) that served the eastern part of New York State. Our team had been focused on the high utilization of healthcare resources by physicians in our network. One individual was an internist in a small rural community in upstate New York. His billing for emergency room visits was excessive. My boss, adamant about putting a stop to this costly emergency utilization, insisted that I have a face-to-face meeting with this doctor to strongly urge him to improve his emergency room use.

I set out on my mission from New York City in mid-afternoon. This was well before the days of GPS, so I was relying on a printed map. By the time I reached the general area of my destination, the sun had gone down, and I found myself on a rural, two-lane road enveloped in darkness. I was going over hill and dale with very few houses along the way. I would see a light in the distance, thinking I had finally reached my destination, only to discover it was a barn.

When I finally reached the doctor's home, we sat down, and I began to go over the utilization numbers. He listened patiently and then proceeded to explain the reasons for the data.

He was the only internist my HMO had recruited into the network of participating doctors in his area. Most of the people enrolled in the HMO in this area worked at the small community hospital. As a physician with admitting privileges to the hospital, he had to cover the emergency room three times a week. Most of his patients, who were also HMO members, knew he would be there, so rather than go to his office, they would show up in the emergency room.

By the time we completed our conversation, I was quite empathetic and thanked him for his commitment to his patients. I knew that empathy and compassion were not enough to change the circumstances under which this physician was functioning. I assured him that recruiting additional physicians to be in the network would be a top priority. The ride home gave me plenty of time to reflect on the importance of finding the root causes of a problem before developing a corrective plan of action.

Unfortunately, the principles of being empathetic while also seeking root causes, which I have tried to apply in my own life, are not a universal constant that can be applied to everyone with equally satisfying results.

LEADER-TO-LEADER CONVERSATIONS

Consider the historical account of the multiple meetings between Britain's Prime Minister Neville Chamberlain and Adolf Hitler that Malcolm Gladwell discusses in his book *Talking to Strangers*.

Chamberlain believed that Hitler actually wanted peace and thus proposed a policy of appeasement toward Hitler. They subsequently signed the Munich Agreement, which Hitler violated several months later. World War II was soon underway.

Chamberlain was not the only one deceived after personal interactions. Lord Halifax, who would later become Chamberlain's foreign secretary, had met with high-level officials of Hitler's regime and was equally convinced that Hitler did not want war, as was another diplomat, Neville Henderson, British ambassador to Germany.

Despite personal meetings with Hitler, Chamberlain's assessment was misguided. In this case, personal experiences do not always reveal the many sides of an individual. Some believe Chamberlain relied solely on the input of those who thought as he did. If Chamberlain had sought the counsel of others such as Winston Churchill and Anthony Eden, who preceded Halifax as foreign secretary, his perception of Hitler may have been quite different. Both Churchill and Eden saw the true character of Hitler and his intentions.

A second possibility notes that perhaps Chamberlain, Halifax, and Henderson were so focused on empathizing with Hitler that they were unable to assess him more objectively. They were anxious to identify common ground for what they thought would establish a stable relationship.

This historical episode is counterintuitive to my original premise of relying on a personal interaction before forming a final impression. There are individuals in this world who are quite adept at deception. They can be polite, empathetic, and appear to be aligned with your thinking, only to act in a way that is beneficial only to them. Validate what is said before you incorporate and move ahead.

FINDING COMMON GROUND

Be genuine in expressing your concern and desire to learn what others are thinking or experiencing. This allows you to identify mutual points of interest and can serve as a foundation to build a more effective relationship.

The concept of finding common ground is certainly worthy of consideration when leaders find themselves engaged in fierce contract negotiations and prolonged strikes. According to the Bureau of Labor Statistics, nearly 500,000 workers went on strike in 2018, an enormous rise from 25,000 in 2017. The trend continued in 2019, with teachers, autoworkers, and supermarket employees finding it necessary to go on strike to have their demands and issues addressed. In 2020 and 2021, 4.3 million workers were engaged in work stoppages. This is driven in part by the increasing cost of living, rising healthcare costs, demands for better working conditions, and greater awareness of executive compensation and corporate profits.

Although the concerns and factors involving each group are varied and complex, the resolution begins with each party finding something on which they can agree. This signals a degree of understanding and valuing each other's position. When you recognize and acknowledge value, you establish a reason to go forward, effectively setting in motion your ability to lead your constituents.

REFERENCES

Bogage J. Strikes Are Sweeping the Labor Market as Workers Wield New Leverage. *The Washington Post*. October 15, 2021. www.washingtonpost.com/business/2021/10/17/strikes-great-resignation.

Gladwell M. *Talking to Strangers: What We Should Know About the People We Don't Know*. New York: Little Brown and Company; 2019.

Kerns Goodwin, D. *Leadership in Turbulent Times*. New York: Simon and Schuster; 2018.

Kerpen D. *The Art of People: 11 Simple People Skills That Will Get You Everything You Want*. New York: Crown Business; 2016.

CHAPTER 10

Motivation

———

*Internal and external forces can inspire
our success or inhibit our progress*

Motivation is the driving force that inspires individuals to be dedicated, creative, and innovative. When you are motivated, you consistently try to be the best you can be.

You understand the vision and proceed with deliberate purpose. You align purpose with your goals. You recognize and embrace the opportunity to add value, experience, knowledge, and insight. You are confident that what you do or say matters, that you are of value. Equally important, you consistently look forward to doing your work, being productive, and helping to make a positive difference. You realize these intrinsic aspects of your character are far greater incentives than the prospect of a higher salary or job promotion.

Studies have shown that monetary incentives, rewards, and other signifiers (pens, paperweights, notebooks with logos, a company party) do not lead to sustained performance improvement. While most people enjoy the company picnic or holiday party, a more enduring affirmation of one's value and work is a personal interaction with one's manager that includes acknowledgment of the quality of an individual's work and contribution to the team. It is most gratifying and motivating when the leader doesn't hesitate to convey these thoughts to others.

Most people like to feel good about what they do and to know that others appreciate their effort. I have tried to follow this practice throughout my career, speaking to every staff member I saw, inquiring about their wellbeing, and asking how the work was proceeding. If I knew they were working on special projects or issues, I discussed their progress or asked if I could be of assistance.

When someone outside our department visited, I thought it was especially important to point to the role an individual played in a particular project or assignment. If someone requested assistance with a particular question or issue, I gladly referred them to the team member with the most insight or experience. My intent was to convey to each team member that I not only knew what they were capable of producing or sharing, but also that I wanted others to see them as mature, competent professionals.

I was delighted when questions on issues such as coding, medical necessity/policy, or new medical technology came into our department and were directed to the individual with the most experience and knowledge on the subject for several reasons:

- My efforts to acknowledge the talents of individual staff members were working.
- Those requesting assistance did not appear to abuse the access to my team by bombarding them with trivial questions.
- The team member who responded consistently provided thorough, well-organized replies expeditiously.
- This process enabled many individuals to make well-informed decisions promptly.

Over time, staff members became more confident, self-directed, and able to lead presentations, meetings, and discussions. They were proud of their work and motivated to improve despite a demanding workload.

INTRINSIC AND EXTRINSIC MOTIVATION

In his article "Stopping the Medical School 'Arms Race'," Vinay Prasad, MD, MPH, shares the story of a high school freshman who applied to work in Prasad's cancer drug/research policy group. Prasad wondered if this request was a genuine expression of this 14-year old's intrinsic motivation or simply a calculated step to prepare an impressive list of activities and accomplishments when he applied to medical school. It raises the question of how much of a developing child's motivation is driven by parental programming of a child's day. This may be part of the nature versus nurture discussion mentioned in Chapter 3 about how we develop and who we become.

Sometimes the most earnest efforts of extrinsic (external) and intrinsic (internal) motivation and support fail to achieve the desired result. This was the case in the life of the intellectually gifted Robert Peace. In his book *The Short and Tragic Life of Robert Peace,* Jeff Hobbs, Robert's Yale roommate, captures the poignant and complex battle between internal and external motivations that shaped Peace's life.

Peace grew up in Newark, New Jersey, a city struggling to recover from the devastating riots in the 1960s. Drugs, violence, and an inferior public education system mirrored the environment of many inner cities around the country. Peace lived with his single mother, who refused to marry his father, who was a drug dealer. Still, Peace's father was very present in his life for the first few years, and the time Peace spent with his mother and father was a joy.

His mother regularly read to him and, determined to send him to private school, enrolled him in a private Catholic school. His father strongly disagreed with this decision. These conflicting views between his parents were part of the many forces that created a powerful battle of competing external and internal motivational influences that would weigh heavily on Peace for the rest of his life.

The positive, nurturing, and motivational experiences were shattered when at the age of seven, Robert learned that his father had been arrested as the prime suspect in a double homicide. Yet, nothing seemed to interfere with Robert's love of books. His early leadership potential was evident as he led academic teams, participated in extracurricular activities, and excelled in sports.

Despite his drinking, smoking marijuana, and maintaining connections with peers in his neighborhood, Robert graduated from high school with a 3.97 GPA. This academic performance, along with his charismatic leadership in student activities, led to his acceptance to Johns Hopkins, Yale, and Penn State universities. All offered partial scholarships, but Peace would have to find a way to make up the difference.

The answer came when after hearing Robert speak at the school banquet, Charles Cawley, the CEO of Maryland Bank National Association (now part of Bank of America), said, "You can go to college wherever you want." Cawley delivered a blank check to pay Robert's tuition and expenses to Yale University.

Cawley's action was an excellent example of the kind of leadership embraced in the **People Value Proposition**.

- He took the time to listen.
- He could appreciate the potential value in the individual.
- He took a definitive step to support the development of the individual.
- He served as a true external motivational force.

Within a few months into his freshman year, Robert realized that the Yale campus would be a lucrative market for selling drugs, and he soon established an endless supply of marijuana to Yale students.

Robert graduated from Yale with a degree in molecular biophysics and biochemistry and returned to Newark to teach biology at St. Benedict's. One would expect that with these many positive external and internal motivational forces, Robert would go on to achieve many notable accomplishments. Unfortunately, this was not the case.

Peace's father died in prison, and five years later, Robert was murdered in his home by a rival drug gang. I believe that Robert's most powerful internal force was to be like his father, someone who was smart enough to communicate with anyone in the streets of their neighborhood and to command their respect. Ironically, it is the same internal force that overshadowed the positive external forces.

The best motivational efforts are negated by the negative power of the streets.

I share the story of Robert Peace to remind leaders that sometimes, even when the person with incredible talent and potential is identified, and you have done everything possible to engage, inspire, and motivate that individual, it may not be enough.

I also share Peace's story because it could have been my story. Like Robert, I spent the first 13 years of my life with my mother in a single-parent family. Although I never knew my father, I longed to know who he was, to be with him.

My first memory of a home that my mother and I shared was a single room in the attic of a boarding house. My mother read to me nearly every night — comic books my mother bought on our way back from visiting relatives.

At the time, I had no idea of the sacrifices my mother, who was employed at a dry-cleaning business, was making to not only take care of our basic needs but also to place me in a daycare program and frequently splurge on a comic book. I was accumulating quite a collection. One evening, I was devastated to discover that someone had broken into our room and stolen all of my comic books. My mother said it was time to move.

My mother and I did not have an apartment of our own. We shared a three-room, cold-water flat with extended family that at one point included 13 individuals. The only toilet (no tub, no shower) was shared with a family on the third floor. This was my home until I graduated from the eighth grade. These were early lessons in managing change, maintaining agility, and understanding resource allocation.

As difficult as these circumstances may sound, I was grateful for a family circle of women who loved, nurtured, and cared for each other and all the children. Unlike Robert's relationship with his father, there was no competing male influence to distract me from the positive structure and expectations my mother and two aunts provided. Their strong religious faith and dedication to family strongly influenced the development of my own values and ethics. To this day, my cousins and I think of each other as brothers and sisters. I was never hungry and always had clothes to wear. I was never late for school because one of my aunts was the official caretaker while the adults went off to work. She never let us oversleep.

I had many teachers who encouraged me to learn and excel. My mother also knew the value of a good education. She purchased an entire set of encyclopedias. I also had access to all the books I could read from my school library and the public library.

Graduation from eighth grade marked a turning point in my life. My mother married a man who would become the only father I have ever known. There was a new leader in our family. He was a hard-working man who worked six days a week and still prepared dinner every Sunday. He was an intelligent man who read the newspaper and loved politics. He loved us all and set the example for what it meant to be a supportive and caring dad.

We moved into a small home. For the first time in our lives, my brother and I had our own beds. I was no longer the man of the house. I spent the next four years adjusting to my new Dad, coping with the developmental tasks of adolescence, and taking on the challenges of high school. It was equally challenging for my brother, who was several years younger. He not only had to deal with a new "alpha male" but also with being frequently compared to his older brother.

Our experience was not unlike employees in an organization trying to adjust to a new leader. My brother and I had to adjust to this new transformational leader while simultaneously trying to establish our own identities and values. By the time I neared graduation from high school, my Dad called me "son."

I was growing up in the small town of Poughkeepsie, New York, 75 miles north of New York City. In addition to the love, structure, and guidance provided at home, there was another place that had a significant impact on my development.

I had a safe and nurturing place to be when I was not in school or at home. I spent most of my free time at the Lincoln Recreation Center (LRC). Through those years, (LRC) provided access to an incredible array of recreational and educational experiences.

One of the most impactful experiences was participating in the LRC Leadership Council. This was a small group of high school students who developed a center newsletter and organized talent shows that attracted people from all areas of the city. We were supervised and guided by staff members who saw value in each of us and did all they could to help us reach our full potential. We raised enough money to send me on a seven-week educational tour across the United States. All of the council members went on to have successful careers. This council experience was a significant motivational force in my life and an early template for becoming a leader.

I had the opportunity to excel in many directions in high school. I participated in various clubs, including a year on the debate team. I graduated in the top third of my class as a solid B student. No one offered a fully paid opportunity to attend college; my Mom and Dad certainly believed in the value of education but had no resources to support a college education. I was convinced that I would not go to college. I turned down a $250 scholarship my church wanted to award me. A positive external motivation negated by a realistic assessment of my family's financial resources.

I decided to follow in the footsteps of a cousin who lived in New York City. He had taken a job as a shipping clerk and went to school at night to become an x-ray technician. I enrolled in the same school and got a job as a shipping clerk in a small tie factory. Apart from the janitor, I was the only other person of color in the entire factory. It was my first full-time employment after high school. The year spent in this job proved to be quite valuable for a number of reasons:

- I earned $48 dollars per week before taxes; careful money management was a skill I quickly acquired.
- I realized that I had a significant role in completing the transaction between the production of ties and their safe delivery to customers.
- I worked with a young salesman who had started as a shipping clerk. He became my mentor and friend.
- The two business owners did not spend their time in an office but rather were present on the shop floor helping to make the ties. They were very supportive and even invited me to their homes for dinner.
- Most of the employees were Jewish women, who soon became my surrogate mothers, offering me something to eat, teaching and encouraging me to go beyond the life of a shipping clerk. To demonstrate her belief in me and my potential, one woman gave me a copy of Grey's Anatomy, a classic textbook used in medical schools.

Collectively, this experience served as a wonderful external motivational source, and like a good leader who exemplifies the **People Value Proposition**, the owners, my mentor, and the women employees inspired me to want to do more and be more than a shipping clerk.

With the blessings of all, I left my job at the tie factory. My internal motivation was further spurred by the fact that I had finished my night course in x-ray technology, only to learn that standards for the field had changed, and I could not get a job as an x-ray technician. I needed a Plan B.

Plan B was even more challenging. I was now married, and my wife and I were expecting our first child. The goal of attending college and the dream of possibly pursuing a career in medicine were rapidly fading. I had a new set of priorities and responsibilities to manage. However, I was fortunate to have parents, in-laws, and a wife, all of whom knew the importance and value of a college education. They all encouraged me not to abandon the idea of going to college. Collectively, they assured me that my family would manage while I pursued a college education — the first in my family to do so.

At this point, a good friend and mentor helped me gain admission to Howard University, an historically black university, where I majored in biology. My time at Howard was a period of life-changing revelations. It was the first time I was aware of so many people of color from all over the world pursuing higher education. The students represented many ethnic and religious groups and spoke many different languages. Each offered a brief glimpse into the diversity and complexity of the world in which we lived. Although I could not appreciate it at the time, this exposure contributed significantly to the development of a strong belief that all people are of value.

After two years, I transferred to Marist College in Poughkeepsie, New York, my hometown. I felt a great need to be reunited with my family and to be a part of their daily lives.

Upon graduating from Marist, like Robert, I returned to my high school to teach biology. Unlike Robert, I was no longer haunted by the absence of my biological father. I was no longer focused on where I came from but where I was going. I had the love, encouragement, and support of family, mentors, and friends, motivating me to pursue a career in Medicine.

I had a wonderful time teaching biology and trying to serve as a mentor and role model. I was motivated more than ever to do more. After I completed 18 months of teaching, I applied for a King-Kennedy pre-med fellowship at the Albert Einstein College of Medicine. I was one of seven students accepted from all areas of the US. The next year I was accepted by three medical schools but chose to stay at Einstein. I now had the opportunity to make my dream a reality.

Robert Peace's intellectual gifts, the support of his mother and mentors, unfortunately, could not alter the trajectory of his life nor change its tragic ending. My journey was not without its challenges but was navigated with the love of my family, the support and guidance of mentors, and the affirmation of my value by colleagues and leaders. My life experiences have taught me that motivation and emotions are woven together in a complex set of circumstances that are unique to each person. A leader's task is to help individuals avoid or manage the threat of one inhibiting the other. The leader may not always be successful, but this is a reality he or she must accept.

REFERENCES

Hobbs J. *The Short and Tragic Life of Robert Peace*. New York: Scribner; 2014.

Prasad V. Stop the Medical School "Arms Race." *Medscape Oncology*. January 31, 2020.

CHAPTER 11

Inspiration and Innovation

———

Inspiration—the source of innovation

"Although I cannot move and I have to speak
through a computer, in my mind I am free"

—STEPHEN HAWKING

An inspiration ignites emotion, imagination, or passion within one's self or others.

Bonuses and free lunch on employee recognition day neither inspire nor encourage innovation. Inspiration and innovation emerge when an individual is fully engaged, takes pride in work accomplished or projects completed, and feels valued and respected for his knowledge, experience, and opinion. Inspiration happens when the breadth of one's knowledge and experience triggers an idea that improves the process and the product.

The desire to do better, be better, and make a positive difference not only for one's self but also for others is an inspiration. I experienced this feeling after graduating from college with a major in biology.

Before getting accepted into the King-Kennedy program, noted in the previous chapter, I considered applying to medical school but was advised to consider graduate school first. Unfortunately, that was the extent of the guidance I received. I had enjoyed the study of anatomy and thought it would be a good path to pursue in graduate school. I applied to two schools and was rejected by both. Strike one!

Despondent, I began to question my own worth. Perhaps this notion of becoming a physician was just a "pipe dream." So, along with many of my high school peers, I thought a job at IBM would be my best bet for earning a living. I interviewed at several IBM locations in the area but was told there were no immediate opportunities. They would keep my application on file. Strike two!

Next, I heard about a possible job as a leader of a Boy Scout troop. The Boy Scouts of America wanted to start a troop for the inner-city youngsters in the city where I grew up. The interview seemed to have gone well, but I was soon notified that I did not get the position. Strike three!

Fortunately, this was not baseball but the beginning of an unpredictable journey through life. The best leaders understand that when one path does not lead to where you need to go, find another. Giving up is not an option.

I could not sit back and feel sorry for myself. The need to support a family and pay rent are powerful motivators. I turned to older friends for advice. I quickly followed through on one suggestion and applied for a position as a substitute teacher in the local school system from which I had graduated a few years earlier. Within a few days, I was called to fill in for a physical education teacher at the high school I had attended. Shortly thereafter, I was asked to substitute for a biology teacher. When the biology teacher returned, I was offered a full-time position in the biology department when a position became available.

Someone thought I was of value. Now I had to prove it to myself. I was determined to make biology, the study of life or living matter, relevant to the lives of my 10th-grade students. I was fresh out of college and excited about the prospect of teaching a well-worn curriculum in innovative ways. I was not trying to inspire my students to become biologists; I simply wanted them to look forward to coming to class and to leave it knowing that biology was about them and every living thing around them.

I experienced one of my most rewarding inspirations when teaching the section on microbiology. I envisioned this subject as a unique opportunity for my students to learn something about themselves and their immediate environment. I wanted the words in the textbook to be understood in a more tangible way.

Several of the boys had physical education before my class. I knew they did not routinely take showers after gym. I gathered some agar plates, a couple of incubators, and some sterile swabs and asked a few of the boys if we could swab their armpits. I showed them how to inoculate the agar plates, label them, and place them in the incubator. I asked other students to make similar cultures by swabbing doorknobs and desktops.

I had a pretty good idea about what we would find the next day when we examined the plates.

At the next class meeting, we pulled out the cultures, which were overgrown with multiple types of bacteria. We now had the opportunity to talk about microbiology in terms of the world around them. We talked about how odor is generated from a lack of personal hygiene and its relationship to the activity of the bacteria they had harvested from their armpits.

The importance of hand washing and how easy it is to be exposed to germs from one's environment was apparent to everyone, as we studied the cultures from the doorknobs and desktops.

This was a day I felt I had done something of value and hopefully inspired a few young minds. I had offered an innovative way to understand microbiology. I cannot say that everyone was now taking showers after gym class, but I think they were at least wiping their armpits with wet paper towels.

I do not know if my approach to teaching inspired my students to go on to become great contributors to society. Nor do I know if the time spent in my classroom had an impact on their lives. I do hope the experience helped some think and explore beyond their comfort zones.

It is likely that teachers and leaders at every level rarely know the impact of what they have said, actions they have taken, or their accomplishments have had on the lives of others. Some notable exceptions are Oprah Winfrey, Desmond Doss, and Stephen Hawking. All have inspired millions and led by example in unique ways.

OPRAH WINFREY

Media mogul, actress, producer, philanthropist. Born in Mississippi, Winfrey was raised by her grandmother during the first few years of her life; then, she lived with various family members. Between the ages of 9 and 13, she was sexually molested by family members.

Winfrey learned to read at the age of three and, in spite of the adversities in her home life, developed into an excellent student. Upon graduating from college, she began a career in radio. She continued to hone her skills in radio and television, ultimately developing a following of 20 million viewers. She continued to expand her influence and ability to inspire others through acting and producing films, publishing, and owning her own television network

With a seemingly endless capacity for empathy, compassion, and genuine caring, Winfrey has connected with millions of people who see her as a leader. She consistently seeks the value in others, supports their development, and facilitates their progress. Much of this is accomplished through her philanthropic support of multiple foundations and charities. For example, she created Project Cuddle, which rescues babies from abandonment and abuse, provides scholarships, finances the construction of schools for children in developing countries, and supports research for AIDS and HIV cures and treatment.

Oprah Winfrey inspires millions and leads by example without issuing a single directive or mandate.

DESMOND DOSS

Seventh-Day Adventist, conscientious objector, Congressional Medal of Honor recipient. Corporal Desmond Doss's inspirational story captures many of the desirable characteristics of a leader.

Doss was raised as a Seventh-day Adventist Christian with a strong belief in the Ten Commandments of the Bible — in particular, the sixth commandment: "Thou Shall Not Kill." When World War II began, Desmond was employed in the Newport News Naval Yard. He could have received a deferment from the military but wanted to do more. He enlisted in the army to be a medical corpsman.

By enlisting as a medic, Doss assumed he would not have to carry a weapon. He was wrong. When he continually refused to carry a weapon, he was ridiculed and castigated by peers and officers. He was considered a liability, and attempts were made to have him court-martialed. All failed to deter him from his determination to serve his country. Through it all, he maintained a calm demeanor and bore no animosity toward his detractors, an extraordinary example of emotional intelligence.

Doss's unit was deployed to the island of Okinawa, where they encountered an enemy force occupying Maeda Escarpment, a cliff several hundred feet high. They initially captured the ridge but subsequently met a fierce counterattack. The US soldiers were sustaining high casualties and were subsequently ordered to retreat back down the wall. All who could retreat did, with the exception of medic Desmond Doss.

Doss knew that many of his fellow soldiers lay severely wounded and dying. He began to retrieve them one by one. He used a rope with an innovative double loop knot he had devised in training to lower each man to his comrades below, managing to save 75 lives.

Of the 16 million soldiers who served in World War II, Desmond Doss was one of only 431 to receive the Congressional Medal of Honor. He is unique in that he never carried a weapon or killed an enemy soldier. He was admired and respected by his fellow soldiers and served as an inspiration for millions.

STEPHEN HAWKING

Theoretical cosmologist, director of research at the Center for Theoretical Cosmology at Cambridge University, teacher, author. At age 21, Stephen Hawking was diagnosed with Amyotrophic Lateral Sclerosis (ALS), a progressive motor neuron disease that destroys all voluntary muscle control. He was ultimately confined to a computerized wheelchair.

He was married twice and was the father of three children, all of whom provided an endless amount of love and support. Hawking ultimately became the quintessential example of one's ability to adapt to change, persevere through the devastating destruction of his body, and simultaneously use his most valuable asset: his mind. He became known for his incredible wit and sense of humor. One of his many notable quotes was, "Intelligence is the ability to adapt to change."

Hawking was able to communicate by using a small sensor controlled by a single muscle in his cheek. He used this mechanism to type on a computer keyboard. In addition to leading research at the Center for Theoretical Cosmology, he authored 16 books that sold 10 million copies. His books have been published in multiple languages. He made countless public appearances throughout the world, never concerned about any limitations or how he appeared to others. He once noted, "Although I cannot move and I have to speak through a computer, in my mind, I am free."

Each of these individuals demonstrates that it is possible to inspire and influence others even when they are not subordinates and are under no obligation to follow your lead. Collectively they illustrate some of the key principles of the **People Value Proposition**:

- Everyone matters; you and they are of value.
- Use the resources you have to help others.

It is difficult to write about inspirational leadership and not think about the thousands of athletes who have provided so many memorable moments in sports, moments that have inspired men, women, and children around the world. I will focus on one who achieved this status in a unique way.

Mike Krzyzewski, coach of the Duke University Blue Devils men's basketball team for more than 40 years, is an excellent example of an inspirational leader. His teams have won more National Collegian Athletic Association (NCAA) Division I games than any other in history. His philosophy of coaching was built on:

- Respect and caring for one another.
- Belief in one's self.
- Constant reassurance.

Coach K, as he is often referred to, recognizes that talent and coaching are essential for a team to be successful, but he firmly believed that "The single most important ingredient after you get the talent is internal leadership, that one person or people on the team who set higher standards than that team would normally set for itself."

Coach K's philosophy and perspective on leadership are applicable to any organization and bring to mind Bill Russell, former center and coach of the Boston Celtics professional basketball team. Russell exemplified the internal leadership Coach K spoke about. He led the Celtics to 11 National Basketball Association (NBA) championships in 13 years. He was not the prolific scorer or the one the coach wanted to take the game-winning shot. He controlled the game defensively and unselfishly. He prevented the other teams from scoring by blocking shots and gathering in offensive and defensive rebounds (averaging 22 per game). Equally important, once he had possession of the ball, he initiated fast breaks (quickly getting the ball to teammates), enabling them to score before the other team could set a defense against them.

Bill Russell and the Boston Celtics were the prototypes for organizational success built on setting and adhering to a high standard. Russell believed in allowing his teammates to utilize their best skills and did all he could to create opportunities for them to use them. They demonstrated the importance of believing in one's self, respecting, caring, and sharing with one another. The internal leadership provided the inspiration and motivation for their success.

When he presented an award to Bill Russell, Kobe Bryant spoke with great reverence, noting Russell's leadership qualities: "vision, trust, and sacrifice."

The individuals described above illustrate a few of the distinct ways in which an individual can be inspired and inspire others. Although each story is unique, the leaders share some common characteristics:

- The ability to overcome adversity and use it to motivate rather than deter one's progress.
- The ability to focus on the immediate task to be completed.
- The ability to convey passion and commitment by doing, not saying.
- The ability to go beyond the limitations and risks to achieve a better outcome.
- The ability to share, sacrifice, or give whatever you have.

INNOVATION

Innovation is inspired by the desire to make life better now and in the future. Innovation is often generated from the knowledge of what currently exists and the ability to envision that which does not.

Innovation within organizations requires leaders who believe "we can do better," who move beyond their own frame of reference. As noted in earlier chapters, they must be open to new ideas, have the courage to risk exploring new approaches and diverse perspectives. This can facilitate the development of a new or improved process, service, or system that accelerates efficiency and effectiveness or helps establish a competitive advantage in the marketplace.

The ability to listen and digest information can lead to a new product or service that can meet an unmet need. Innovations are not always radical or disruptive in the marketplace. They may be incremental or structurally different and still be viewed as new and desirable.

The key components for the success of any innovation are similar to those applied to a marketing strategy, product development, or communication initiative for any business or industry. A business leader learns as much as possible about a potential customer by asking questions such as:

- What is the social and economic profile of the customer?
- What are the primary needs or desired services?
- What are the organization's capabilities to deliver the services or meet the needs?
- What data are needed to assure the best quality product or services are produced?
- What are the best mechanisms for engaging and communicating with the customer?

To answer these questions, the organization collects and analyzes data and determines how to use them, stratifies the needs to prioritize the allocation of resources, and addresses these needs while achieving better outcomes at a lower cost.

Real change is occurring in several areas.

Genomic medicine, the ability to understand various conditions at the molecular genetic level (21,000 genes on 23 pairs of chromosomes), has led to great advances in understanding what defines us as unique individuals. Genomics has significantly impacted our lives in many ways, according to the NIH National Human Genome Research Institute:

- Detecting, treating, and preventing a wide variety of diseases and conditions caused by bacteria and viruses.
- Transforming the way in which we study, diagnose, and treat cancer.
- Helping to choose the right medication, at the right dose for each patient, through pharmacogenomics.
- Utilizing non-invasive prenatal testing to detect conditions such as Down syndrome.
- Enhancing the ability of forensic scientists to identify causes of previously unexplained events.

The internet has greatly enhanced our lives. You can now shop on the internet, purchase anything from underwear to automobiles, and have it delivered to your doorstep. Family members spread across a continent can now see and speak with each other through Zoom and Facebook internet services. The internet has become the primary source to find information on anything and everything, although it is also a primary source of misinformation and deception.

Innovation is a critical factor in facilitating progress and implementing change. Leaders have a responsibility to understand the history or evolution of what is considered an innovation. This is essential to understanding what is new or previously unknown. Leaders are then able to determine where and how to focus resources to achieve a better outcome. Thus, they avoid doing the same thing that has been done and then expecting different results. They can use innovations to effect real change.

REFERENCES

Bass B.M. *Leadership and Performance Beyond Expectations*. New York: Free Press; 1985.

Gladwell M. *Outliers: The Story of Success*. New York: Little Brown and Company; 2008.

Manolio TA, Bult CJ, et. al. Genomic Medicine Year in Review: *The American Journal of Human Genetics*. 2019;105:1072-1075.

National Institutes of Health, National Human Genome Research Institute. https://www.genome.gov/dna-day/15-ways

CHAPTER 12

Leading Change

—

*Take the action that makes a
difference, change the norm*

In an earlier chapter, I shared my transition from a primary care pediatrician to director of a multidiscipline community healthcare center. I described how my senior staff and I had to lead change in order to establish a culture built around the **People Value Proposition**. Throughout the rest of my professional career, I have had numerous opportunities to think about the necessity of change, the complexity of change, and the challenges of leading change.

THE NECESSITY OF CHANGE

As a parent and pediatrician, I am acutely aware of the necessary changes every human must experience in their growth from infancy to adulthood. Not every individual makes the transition from one phase of the lifecycle to the next with the same degree of confidence, trust, or willingness to change. Human development and maturation offer some interesting insights and parallels to understanding the complexities of change and the challenges of leading change.

The following thoughts are not intended to trivialize the changes one can encounter in pursuit of a meaningful work experience. They merely represent one perspective on leaders and employees seen through the eyes of a pediatrician.

Consider the toddler about to be weaned from the nipple (natural or artificial) to the sippy cup and eventually to solid food. The greater the sense of security and comfort derived from the breastfeeding or bottle-feeding experience, the more difficult it is to move on to the next stage. The resistance can be fierce at times. I've seen a toddler literally tear at a mother's clothing to suckle on her breast. The toddler is not hungry; he just wants to experience that sense of warmth and security after a stressful day at daycare.

Now consider the employee who has been informed that his job description has changed. He will have new responsibilities and must acquire new skills to fulfill them. To effectively lead this change, the leader, like a mother, must begin by anticipating the anxiety generated by completely disrupting the comfort zone of the employee/child. She must be patient, provide the necessary tools, educate, reassure, and guide to enable the employee to move forward.

As the child continues to develop, learning to share and to care about others are important steps in developing relationships and bonds with classmates. These relationships are key facilitators of a child's transition from home to classroom, toward accepting and managing change. Similarly, the employee's relationship with peers and leaders helps him move from resisting change to accepting, if not embracing, change.

To be clear, none of these steps can be viewed as "a one size fits all" concept. Each employee has a unique set of experiences, emotions, and expectations that influence the degree of resistance or acceptance and its manifestation. These factors determine who follows passively and who becomes an active participant.

Despite the underlying drivers of resistance or acceptance, the leader must adequately frame and explain the necessity for change. The leader must listen to concerns and determine what is most important to those who resist. Whenever possible, the leader should address those concerns openly and honestly and resist becoming bogged down in verbal sparring that consumes valuable time.

The effective leader helps those who are willing to follow and possibly lead to clearly understand the need for change and how it will be accomplished. Clarity and rationale, as well as the valued contribution of an employee, are strong incentives for adaptation or implementation of change.

THE COMPLEXITY OF CHANGE

A leader must continue to emphasize the value of the individual. She must constantly assert that applying one's skills, sharing knowledge, and caring about colleagues relate to individual success, the success of the team, and, ultimately, the success of the organization.

When children enter pre-school, the transition from "me" to "us" begins. They learn to share toys and put them away when it is time for the next activity. They participate in clean-up after a creative session of finger painting. When they get out the musical instruments (triangles, tambourines, and tom-toms) for an invigorating jam session, they are experiencing the rudimentary act of trying to create something in unison, the early foundation for teamwork. When children are sitting quietly, listening to a story read by the teacher, looking for the buddy whose hand must be held as they march out to the playground, this is the beginning of sharing and working cooperatively with others.

As a child's mental and physical skill sets develop, so does the ability to appreciate the value of others. This is especially true in team sports, extracurricular activities, boys' and girls' scout troops, and community service projects. They share with others the emotional joy of winning or disappointment of losing. Each experience offers the prospect of learning from mistakes and doing better. Each success reinforces the idea that hard work and dedication can be rewarding and that much can be accomplished when people act in unison, visualize a goal, and set out to accomplish it together.

Young people who are engaged in a team activity or a solo activity, such as playing chess, performing a solo dance, or using their allowance to pay for another student's school lunch, have been guided and nurtured by a parent, teacher, mentor, or coach. Effective leaders can have a similar impact on adults in the workplace.

The adult whose job has thrust new demands on both body and mind can benefit from a leader or mentor who explains the reasoning behind the new responsibilities and provides access to the skills or knowledge to support these changes. Change may require working with new team members or interdepartmental collaboration and establishing the relationships that will most facilitate accomplishing certain tasks.

As adolescents must establish and navigate social, emotional, and functional relationships, selecting clubs to join, teams to try out for, and classes to take help to shape their vision of who they are and who they hope to be. Parents, guidance counselors, and teachers have a role in leading these changes.

Peer groups also play a major role in this decision-making process. Peers influence how, where, and when to study. They help determine participation in extracurricular activities, attendance at parties, and even dating choices. In the end, however, as they transition from adolescence to adulthood, young people must believe in themselves; they must understand their value and be willing to share it with others.

The changes a working adult may experience in the course of a career are as disruptive and at the same time exhilarating as those changes experienced in adolescence, and they bring to mind the same questions: *Of what value am I? Who cares about me? Where do I fit in? Who do I have a good relationship with? Will our team survive?* These questions require thoughtful and direct responses from leaders.

A parent's job is to nurture a child, to provide reassurance based on life's lessons and knowledge of their world. The parent listens to understand the child's perspective and, when possible, acknowledges its validity. The parent identifies the major influences in a child's life and provides guidance on how to manage them and changes that are to come.

These considerations in the maturing, evolving child offer some parallels to the changes necessary for the evolving organization.

Similar to a parent, a leader must listen, engage, and empathize. When appropriate, the leader must validate an individual's perspective, as well as provide feedback and direction for a more appropriate course of action. The movement from the current state to an uncertain future state that is necessary to ensure viability and improve functionality defines the necessity of change. It also involves determining the best way to effect that change.

Each organization must determine which of many change models will best suit its culture and needs. One of the most widely used is the Kurt Lewin model for organizational change. It begins with the leader's willingness to change the organization's current state. Next is the critical step of facilitating employee involvement in change by sharing knowledge with them and engaging them in the change process. Once that process is implemented, the organizational change is solidified.

A leader must articulate the fundamental practices that support the necessity of change and the imperative to evolve. These practices include:

- Identify the key drivers in the environment that necessitate change.
- Listen to understand the concerns of those who are expected to implement change.
- Be prepared to answer questions as directly and succinctly as possible. Don't be reluctant to say, "I don't know."
- Be prepared with an implementation strategy that allows input from those who will lead the change.
- Facilitate and empower those expected to lead by providing accurate and focused direction.
- Provide reassurance that proven practices that work well will not be automatically discarded. Emphasize that success or complacency will not deter the implementation of change necessary to remain competitive.

These practices distinguish between acting with a sense of urgency and strategic focus versus responding with a chaotic, crisis-driven mindset that results, at best, in a temporary fix. At its worst, chaos breeds disfunction, inefficiency, and lack of confidence in a leader.

THE CHALLENGES OF LEADING CHANGE

These principles provide a framework for an orderly transition into a new functional state. This distinction was of paramount importance to me in the early 1990s. I was assigned to introduce physicians and members of our entire hospital network to a new set of utilization management guidelines.

The Millimen Care Guidelines were being adopted rapidly by health insurance payers and hospitals across the United States. The guidelines were developed from solid, evidence-based data and research. They had already been proven to result in more appropriate hospital admissions and lengths of stay. Now, it was time to introduce them to the physicians and hospitals in our state.

As l prepared to embark on this odyssey to the hospitals in our network, I knew that physicians and hospital administrators would resent a health insurance plan that tried to tell them how to care for their patients. I fully expected hostility at my presentations and joked with colleagues that I would be accompanied by three nurses at every presentation: one to help me distribute the stack of information about the guidelines, one to stand by the nearest exit, and one to wait in the car with the engine running just in case we needed to make a quick getaway.

Invariably, after I was introduced, two or three physicians would immediately begin to vent their frustration and anger with health insurers. I would ask, "How many other insurance companies have a representative who meets with you face to face to explain what they were doing and why?" This question was followed by dead silence. I then knew I could proceed with the presentation.

- My primary responsibility was to inform those who would be followers and leaders of change rather than focus on those who were most resistant to change. When physicians were ranting at the beginning of my presentation, I remained calm because I did not want to get into a shouting match that might convey an attempt to suppress or deny their concerns.
- I wanted to listen to their comments and use their concerns to better prepare for the next presentation.
- By my demeanor, I intended to establish a collegial, information-sharing process that would facilitate change.

At the end of each session, one or two doctors would thank me and express their appreciation for the presentation. It was at those moments that I knew I was successfully leading change.

REFERENCES

Angood P. *All Physicians Are Leaders: Reflections on Inspiring Change Together for Better Healthcare*. Washington, D.C. American Association for Physician Leadership; 2020.

Bossidy L. and Charan R. *Execution: The Discipline of Getting Things Done*. New York: Crown Business; 2002.

Hussain ST, Lei S, et. al. Kurt Lewn's Change Model: A Critical Review of the Role of Leadership and Employee Involvement in Organizational Change. *Journal of Innovation and Knowledge*. 2018; 3:123-127

Kotter J and Rathgeber H. *Our Iceberg Is Melting: Changing and Succeeding Under Any Conditions*. Chicago: Macmillan; 2005.

Ristino R. *The Agile Manager's Guide to Managing Change*. Bristol, VT.: Velocity Business Publishing; 2000.

CHAPTER 13

Transformational Leadership

———

How to get an organization from where it is to where it needs to be

The term *transformational leadership* has been in the leadership lexicon since the 1970s when it was first introduced by sociologist J.V. Downton. Later, James MacGregor Burns defined transformational leadership in his book *Leadership* as "A process in which leaders and their followers raise one another to higher levels of morality and motivation." Since then, the meaning of the term has expanded.

Bernard Bass, in his book *Leadership and Performance Beyond Expectations*, identified four major components of transformational leadership:

1. Inspirational motivation. The leader frames a vision and models the behavior to achieve it. The leader inspires and motivates by providing access to skills development, knowledge, and opportunity.
2. Individualized consideration. The leader seeks the value in individuals, supports, nurtures, and helps them enhance that value.
3. Intellectual stimulation. The leader challenges followers to think, explore, and risk pursuing ideas beyond what they currently know.
4. Idealized Influence. The leader exhibits ethical and moral behavior that generates trust, respect, and pride in everything the followers do.

Kark and colleagues offer an interesting assessment of transformational leadership in their *Journal of Applied Psychology* article, "The Two Faces of Transformational Leadership: Empowerment and Dependency." They cite an apparent paradoxical finding in transformational leadership framed by the followers' dependence on the leader through personal identification and simultaneous empowerment of followers through social identification. Empowerment, by definition, contributes to a sense of self-worth, collective efficacy, and organizational pride.

I, however, do not think of the outcomes of transformational leadership as contradictory or paradoxical. From my perspective, these are the desired outcomes for an organization to function at optimal efficacy and efficiency. My definition of transformational leadership is simple. Transformational leadership takes an organization from where it is to where it has to be in a competitive and evolving environment. Transformational leaders understand and embrace many of the tenets of The People Value Proposition.

TRANSFORMATIONAL LEADERS

Transformational leaders understand the current environment and have a vision of the future. They acknowledge that the core strategic objectives are not sufficient to sustain the continued growth of an organization. Transformational leaders understand the importance of retaining the core business and values but also recognize that these elements may need to be reconfigured or realigned with new initiatives.

To begin the transformation process, leaders augment their own knowledge base and experiences with relevant data and evaluate all potential approaches offered by team members. The leader then makes the definitive decision about new directions to pursue.

Transformational leaders want to be accountable for making the major decisions, but they also want their followers to be prepared and confident in their ability to lead necessary change. The leaders influence, inspire, and empower followers by enabling them to take ownership, exercise initiative, and lead. They inform all members of the management team of the changes to be implemented and why. Managers must be confident and optimistic about the vision and understand the strategy to achieve it. They are the frontline of leadership who will execute the strategic plan.

Once the organization embarks on the transformation, the leader must be prepared to mitigate or manage several issues:

- Anticipate opposition and know how to modify or eliminate it.
- Understand the emotional reactions of team members and acknowledge them.
- Insist on mutual respect and professional decorum.
- Defuse pressure points and maintain equilibrium.
- Monitor progress and recalibrate directions when necessary.

- Remain focused on the primary goal.
- Keep promises.
- Be available and accessible.

In their paper *What the Best Transformational Leaders Do,* Anthony and Schwartz describe a study of S&P 500 and Global 500 firms to identify the companies that have undergone the most successful transformations and the leaders who led them. Fifty-seven companies were initially identified and subsequently reduced to 10 using the following metrics:

- New growth achieved by creating new products, services, and business models that generated revenue above that derived from the core business.
- Repositioning or adapting core business.
- Financial performance during transformation period compared to industry benchmarks.
- Exemplary strategic transformation.
- An impact on customers and its respective industry.
- Showed potential to sustain its transformation.

The 10 finalist companies and their leaders were:

Amazon. *Jeff Bezos, CEO.* Created new growth that was 10% of total revenue. This was accomplished with cloud services, which provide on-demand access to data storage, applications, and other computer system resources through the internet, without direct management by the user.

Netflix. *Reed Hastings, CEO.* Generated new growth that accounted for 80% of total revenue through the introduction of video streaming.

Priceline. *Jeff Boyd & Glenn Fogel, former and current CEO.* Developed new business models in the travel reservations market that accounted for a 25% growth of total revenue.

Apple. *Steve Jobs & Tim Cook former and current CEO.* Innovations of the iPhone & iPad accounted for 80% of total revenue.

Aetna. *Mark Bartolini, CEO.* Initiation of a value-based healthcare concept that pays for care based on quality, outcomes, and lower costs rather than just fee for service, accounted for 40% of total revenue.

Adobe. *Shantanu Narayen, CEO.* Digital marketing strategy accounted for 45% of total revenue.

DaVita. *Kent Thiry, CEO.* Development of a new culture focused on employee engagement and an integrated delivery network of healthcare that would provide a full range of healthcare using the value-based payment model. This transformation to total patient care now accounts for 30% of total revenue.

Microsoft. *Satya Nadella, CEO.* Like Amazon, entered the cloud services market, that now accounts for 32% of total revenue.

Danone. *Emmanuel Faber, CEO.* transformed a company focused on food and beverages to one with a strong commitment to family health and medical nutrition. This transformation now accounts for 29% percent of total revenue.

Krupp Thyssent. *Heinrich Hiesinger, CEO.* Transformed the company by eliminating less profitable products and focused on developing new industrial solutions such as 3D printing centers. This transformation now accounts for 47% of total revenue.

These examples illustrate the broad range of industries in which transformations have been led by extraordinary leaders. It should be noted that while these organizations have undergone successful transformations, it does not mean they are perfect. Some have experienced significant issues such as employee equity and diversity of leadership.

Amazon is a "prime" example. Until the hiring of Alicia Boler Davis as vice president of global customer fulfillment in 2019, Amazon's senior leadership team was composed of mostly White males. Davis's appointment made her only the fourth woman to join this elite group and the first Black woman.

ATTRIBUTES OF TRANSFORMATIONAL LEADERS

All of these companies were led by transformational leaders with several common attributes:

- Each had an average of 14 years of experience with the core business before being offered the CEO position.
- Each had an opportunity to evaluate emerging growth business or to explore external possibilities.
- They all understood that a successful transformation required a repositioning of the core business while simultaneously investing in new growth business.

- They also knew that a successful transformation would require infusing into the organization's culture a willingness to take risks and explore new opportunities.
- Each of these leaders was able to utilize, to different degrees, the four components of Bass's transformational leadership. They could provide inspirational motivation, seek and accept individual ideas and contributions, and act with high moral and ethical standards.

In addition to these attributes, the transformational leader is responsible for defining the key drivers of transformation for an organization and creating the environment that will activate them.

KEY DRIVERS FOR TRANSFORMATION

Exploration. Through exploration, the transformational leader engages the workforce to investigate multiple possibilities while maintaining the stability of the core business. Satya Nadella, the CEO of Microsoft, illustrates the point.

Nadella, who had been with Microsoft since 1992, became CEO in 2014. He understood the importance of mobilizing the intellectual resources of the workforce and knew how to engage and motivate employees. He motivated them, not by giving charismatic speeches but by listening, learning, and analyzing. He then empowered employees to work on projects they were passionate about. This employee engagement led to Microsoft gaining a prominent position in the marketplace for cloud technology services and artificial intelligence, accounting for nearly a third of Microsoft's revenue.

The exploration was accompanied by the opportunity for new ideas to be articulated, assessed, and developed. The confluence of cloud services has revolutionized the way organizations store, access, and utilize data to manage their businesses.

Infusing change into the culture. The transformational leader realizes that communicating a vision for transformation requires framing the messages to the level of each constituent's engagement, comprehension, and responsibilities. The leader must identify those who will be the agents (leaders or facilitators) of change and keep these agents informed, provide appropriate resources, and mitigate any obstacles. In addition, the leader must be prepared to help employees adapt to change and to take on new responsibilities.

In these messages, the leader's knowledge and experience will enable her to frame a realistic strategic plan and emphasize that a transformation is not an overnight phenomenon. It may take years to accomplish and must be embedded in the organization's culture. This requires continuous reinforcement of strategic objectives and when necessary, modification of the strategic plan.

Taking Risks. An organization and leader's ability to take risks is an important factor in achieving a successful transformation. A major risk may entail replacing a CEO or other senior executives, repositioning the core business, or eliminating certain lines of business or products. The decision to expand into new lines of business that may or may not be related to a core business or the development of an entirely new product are also risks. Additional risks may be in the form of outsourcing certain functions or services. Risks may initially incur new costs but, when thoughtfully executed, yield benefits that greatly exceed those costs. Regardless of the nature of risks taken, they are an essential component of an organizational transformation.

Sustained Engagement. Successful transformation requires leaders to sustain engagement at all levels of an organization. To do that, they must connect with employees. In earlier chapters, I described the importance of engaging followers as much a possible on an interpersonal level. Today, employees are increasingly physically separated from each other and from their leaders. Digital technology has become an essential driver to help bridge that gap. Not only does digital technology facilitate connectivity, it also improves the efficiency and accuracy of communications and operations.

Digital Transformation. The 10 finalist transformational companies and their leaders used the key driver of digital transformation in several ways to gather data, analyze it, and redefine the direction of their organizations. Paul Miller, CEO and founder of the Digital Workplace Group and co-author of *The Digital Renaissance of Work,* notes, "Building digital literacy and digital intelligence is foundational to modern successful leadership." Leaders who understand the multiple pathways for using digital technology see the value, justification, and necessity for substantial investment in this technology.

According to IDC Technologies, a leading technology services organization, 40% of all technology spending will be allocated to digital transformation. This is expected to exceed $2.3 trillion annually through 2023. The need to connect, coordinate, and collaborate extends beyond a leaders' followers.

The leader must also ensure that interactions with vendors, contractors, and suppliers of essential services are efficiently managed and monitored. In addition, timely and accurate interactions with regulators, investors, and customers are vital to an organization's survival.

Cybersecurity has become another area of major concern for every leader and organization. A breach of confidential information can be devastating to an organization, undermining customers' trust and confidence. A single cyber intrusion can result in the loss, corruption, or distribution of critical information. This, in turn, can disrupt the entire operation of an organization. Notwithstanding this potential threat, technology has become an indispensable component of every organization.

Today, the United States and much of the developed world are experiencing the most remarkable transformation since the industrial revolution. We live in a world of interstate, regional, national, and global economies. Communication, connectivity, and precise execution are critical requirements for sustaining the viability of transformational organizations. International meetings are often held via teleconferences. A person can purchase an item on the internet today and have it delivered to their doorstep tomorrow. Through social media and internet connectivity, the smallest businesses can establish a thriving customer base with people they have never met nor spoken to directly.

Huge amounts of data are continuously gathered and used to examine every aspect of our lives. These data not only reveal who we are, where we live, and how we shop, but also chronicle our eating, drinking, reading, and other habits or preferences. Companies use this information to develop personalized messaging intended to inspire more consumer spending or to enhance receptivity, absorption, and response to various enticements.

More than ever, businesses must have a customer-centric focus, constantly assessing customer satisfaction and doing it all at a lower cost.

Transformational leaders who can effectively organize, motivate, and lead an organization to integrate the key drivers of transformation into its culture will be essential to the survival of many organizations. The dynamics of commercial and industrial markets continue to evolve rapidly. Some degree of transformation will be necessary. Leaders with transformational attributes will make it possible.

REFERENCES

Boulton C. What Is Digital Transformation? A Necessary Disruption. CIO. June 24, 2021. https://www.cio.com/article/230425/what-is-digital-transformation-a-necessary-disruption.html.

Kark R, Shamir B, and Chen G. The Two Faces of Transformational Leadership: Empowerment and Dependency. *Journal of Applied Psychology.* 2003; 88(2):246-255

Miles R, Leading Corporate *Transformation: A Blueprint for Renewal.* San Francisco: Jossey-Bass Publishers; 1997.

Miller P. My 4 Principles of Digital Leadership. LinkedIn. 2016. www.linkedin.com/pulse/my-4principles-digital-leadership-p

Welch J. *Jack: Straight from the Gut.* New York: Warner Books; 2001.

Anthony SD and Schwartz EI. What the Best Transformational Leaders Do. *Harvard Business Review.* 2017. https://hbr.org/2017/05/what-the-best-transformational-leaders-do

CHAPTER 14

Cultural Humility, Linguistic and Cultural Competence

A universal mandate for every organization

To achieve optimal efficiency and sustained quality, the leader must know the people doing the work. In Chapter 18, I address the importance of knowing staff. It is equally important to be aware of the cultural needs, customs, and expectations of clients with whom an organization does business.

Cultural humility and linguistic and cultural competence should be an intrinsic part of the core values of every organization. Competence in these areas should be viewed as a continuous journey rather than a destination. They are critical elements to remaining competitive and connected in any business or service.

CULTURAL HUMILITY

Cultural humility is a first step in the journey toward cultural literacy and competence. It requires one to develop a deliberate consciousness that involves self-awareness and introspection. Much like emotional intelligence, one must acknowledge one's implicit and unconscious biases or preconceived ideas of others. Then, humility becomes the force that enables one to commit to a lifetime of learning about one's self and understanding others.

Tervalon and Murray-Garcia described three key elements that facilitate the development of cultural humility:

1. Accept that understanding one's self and learning about others, appreciating differences, and respecting them is a continuous journey.
2. Continuously work to recognize the value of every individual. This fosters mutual respect, the sharing of ideas, and the development of empathy.

85

3. Support the development of alliances and partnerships to help and advocate for others.

Cultural humility must be lived before one can begin to gain cultural literacy and competence. A failure to know and understand key principles and behaviors of employees, potential customers, or clients can easily result in offending the client, creating an atmosphere of distrust, or exhibiting a lack of respect.

Knowing means:

- Understanding the cultural imperatives for each identifiable group.
- Empathizing with these groups.
- Accommodating their critical needs.
- Communicating in language best understood by the intended audience.
- Recognizing that respect, trust, and appreciation are best demonstrated by personal interaction.

Know the people you want to lead.

For several days in 2016, Pope Francis visited Mexico, the second-largest Catholic country in the world. Eighty-six percent of Mexico's 113 million people are Catholic. Clearly, the Pope would be speaking to the faithful.

Born in Argentina, Pope Francis speaks fluent Spanish. During his visit, he celebrated many Masses from Mexico City to Chiapas to Juarez. It would appear that the Pope's ability to communicate with his audiences in their native language would not be a problem.

However, all was not as perfectly aligned as hoped. Fortunately, the Pope had an excellent advance preparation staff who discovered that in one of the areas where the Pope would celebrate Mass, the people spoke only an ancient Mayan language, not Spanish. An interpreter was secured, and a major failure to communicate, inspire, and uplift the people was avoided.

This one example underscores the importance of understanding and practicing cultural competence regarding those whom one leads. Cultural competence is relevant in workplaces that want to be identified as equal opportunity employers with a diverse workforce, as well as corporations that intend to compete in a global marketplace.

PRACTICE CULTURAL AND LINGUISTIC COMPETENCE

Cultural and linguistic competence is an integral part of an organization's culture. Cultural competence refers to a concerted effort to recognize and respectfully engage individuals of various cultures, races, ethnicities, languages, belief systems, and other social determinants through a process that maintains dignity and mutual respect. Linguistic competence is the system of rules that govern an individual's tacit understanding of what is acceptable and not acceptable in the language they speak. This knowledge extends beyond grammatical correctness, pronunciation, inflection, and even local dialects. It includes respectfully addressing an individual by name and appropriate title and does not generalize or place anyone in a pluralistic category such as "you people."

Linguistic competence is a critical corollary to cultural competence because it is the primary manner in which intent and comprehension are conveyed. It communicates to the person a level of respect and a depth of understanding of what is important to that individual. Your intentions may be good, but if your demeanor or body language conveys disdain or impatience, you will not communicate effectively or respectfully.

I have spent many years training, working, and living in the north and south communities of the Bronx, one of the boroughs of New York City. I thought I was fairly capable of communicating with individuals from all levels of society and cultural backgrounds until the day I was sitting in a small fast-food restaurant just a few tables away from two young African-American men engaged in an audible conversation. To my surprise, I was unable to understand anything they were saying. It wasn't a foreign language but rather a series of words, interrupted phrases, and slang. The linguistics were unique to these young men and to the context of their day-to-day lives.

Thinking about the context of words in one's life reminded me of two words that, when directed to me, trigger a great deal of frustration or resentment. They are most often uttered by gas station attendants and store clerks who are serving me: "chief" and "boss" in the context of "What can I do for you Chief?" or "Thank you, Boss." Since I am neither a chief nor a boss to these people, as an African-American man over age 40, I think of these words, in this context, as derogatory. I think of all the movies and work situations when I've heard men of color referred to as chief or boss when they were neither. The words were meant to be demeaning, not complimentary or respectful.

This example indicates the ease with which language can fail to communicate effectively.

It is not always the words spoken directly to you that convey a lack of cultural competence; it may simply be the insistence of a leader that you position yourself in a place so you will be seen by an external party. A personal experience illustrates the point.

I was attending an important video conference where I was the only African-American. Our leader felt it was important for me to sit up front so I could be clearly seen by the outside participant. In certain circumstances, being seated in front of an audience could be an honor. In this instance, however, I felt I was being used to make the point, "See, we are a diverse organization."

It is unrealistic to expect everyone to be knowledgeable or sensitive to the nuances of language and actions that are offensive to a person of color, members of the LGBTQ communities, individuals with mental and physical disabilities, as well as other marginalized groups. These sensitivities and points of pain for people in these groups are the result of accumulated experiences over a lifetime and the collective ignorance of others, not a single incident. We can all do a better job of communicating with linguistic and cultural competence. It begins with the commitment to cultural humility.

Practicing cultural humility, linguistic and cultural competence are essential to navigating cross-cultural differences and building an organizational culture that embraces the **People Value Proposition**.

It is not realistic to expect an individual or organization to know every belief, principle, or practice that exists across all cultures. Rather, the goal should be to respect diversity and commit to a continuous process of understanding, acknowledging, and incorporating cultural diversity into the fabric of organizational culture.

In addition, a concerted effort must be made to acknowledge and manage implicit bias and to commit to employing individuals from diverse backgrounds in all levels of leadership.

THE GEORGETOWN MODEL

The National Center for Cultural Competence at Georgetown University suggests the Kolb and Kolb model of experiential learning as an integrated approach to developing cultural and linguistic competence in an organization. The model consists of four major components that can be used in the context of an organization and its leadership:

1. **Concrete experience.** Exploring and attempting to understand the previous experiences, beliefs, and values of employees helps leaders reconsider their thought process and possibly redefine a position when presented with new information or perspectives.
2. **Abstract conceptualization.** The effective use and incorporation of new ideas and information may require framing them in new concepts and context for the employee.
3. **Reflective observation.** This requires the leaders and organization to do honest and thorough self and organizational assessments. This is followed by determining what cultural knowledge and skills need to be acquired, how diversity will be valued, and how cultural and linguistic competence will be embedded in organizational culture.
4. **Active experimentation.** Once the relevance of these competencies is understood and embraced, the organization must empower the leaders and employees to explore new ways to make their new knowledge and perspectives a reality.

These four components must be conducted in a repetitive, integrative process that is subject to modification as needed. These modifications may involve:

- Knowledge of and involvement in diverse communities.
- An organization's long-term commitment and provision of appropriate resources.
- Human resource policies that are committed to obtaining and maintaining a diverse workforce.

The importance of cultural and linguistic competence is widely recognized as an essential element to successfully doing business with diverse communities. The successful development of these competencies is time- and resource-intensive. It requires a leader who is truly dedicated to ensuring that the necessary resources and support are available to execute the task.

CULTURAL AND LINGUISTIC STANDARDS IN HEALTHCARE

In the field of healthcare, understanding cultural and linguistic competence is increasingly important in light of state and federal legislation. For example, the U.S. Department of Health and Human Services issued *National Standards for Culturally and Linguistically Appropriate Services (CLAS) in Health and Health Care: A Blueprint for Advancing and Sustaining CLAS Policy and Practice*

Some of the key objectives in these standards include:

- Eliminating long-standing disparities in the health status of people of diverse racial, ethnic, and cultural backgrounds.
- Improving the quality of services and primary care outcomes.
- Meeting legislative, regulatory, and accreditation mandates.
- Gaining a competitive edge in the marketplace.

At least five states — Washington, California, New Jersey, Connecticut, and New Mexico — require cultural competency training for healthcare providers with each license renewal. This training includes the importance of understanding the patient's deeply engrained beliefs about causes of illness, reasons for disease, and the value or efficacy of treatment approaches. Understanding and acknowledging the patient's perspective can significantly affect one's ability to effectively care for a patient.

During my years of practice in the South Bronx, it was not uncommon to see an infant of a Latino family who would be considered a "failure to thrive." This preliminary diagnosis would be based on an assessment of the child's height, weight, and developmental milestones, all of which were below the standards for a child of comparable age. For a pediatrician, this condition necessitates taking a thorough history and possibly ordering an extensive diagnostic workup.

The possibilities of "failure to thrive" could range from poor dietary intake to a problem with any of the major organ systems to child neglect or abuse. Because my command of Spanish was minimal, I would request an interpreter, fluent in Spanish, even if the patient spoke English.

Before I could begin with my clinical questions, it was important to know if the parent thought the child's condition was the result of *mal de ojo* (evil eye), a hex placed on the child by some envious person. If so, there would be a great deal of empathizing and careful explanations through the interpreter before any work could proceed.

This was the approach I used with the 13-month-old child and mom during their initial visit to my office. Once I knew the age of the child, observed his physical appearance and level of activity, it was apparent he was not developing within the norms for a child his age.

We began the interview slowly, asking the child's mother for her thoughts on the child's appearance, whether she noticed anything different in the child's behavior or activity compared to her other children. The mom responded that yes, this child was smaller, more irritable, and less active than her other children were at this age. We then asked if she knew of any reason the child appeared this way. Without hesitation, she said, "no." At this point, we felt confident that mom was not concerned about an evil external force being responsible for her toddler's condition.

The mother was now quite comfortable with us, and we were able to proceed with a careful history and physical exam. We discovered that several months ago, the family had traveled to their native home in Central America. We conducted several tests that revealed the child had a parasitic infection that we were able to treat, and the child began to thrive.

Our practice of cultural and linguistic competence, in this case, allowed us to communicate in the mother's native language. Moreover, we did not dismiss or minimize the possible belief by a mom that the child was the victim of the "evil eye." Cultural and linguistic competence enabled us to achieve our primary objective to improve the health and well-being of the child. We also established mutual trust and respect, essential to providing excellent patient care. Every customer or client, regardless of cultural or ethnic background, wants to be respected and to believe the organization that he is doing business with can be trusted. This is imperative for the continued viability of any business.

The organizational culture and linguistic competence of an organization's employees determine the effectiveness of its interaction with patients, clients, or customers. A leader's ability to understand and appreciate the influence of cultural norms, religious beliefs, ethnic culture, social-economic and functional perspectives of its staff is critical to achieving business objectives.

Even without a specific mandate, many leaders and organizations have been proactive in providing such training to their employees. The goal is to create greater awareness, sensitivity, and appreciation of the sometimes subtle but often significant differences in the people they want to function as a cohesive team or to serve customers most effectively.

By providing training sessions on cultural diversity, establishing cultural affinity groups, and offering cafeteria menus that offer selections suitable for most cultural dietary needs, employers make an earnest commitment to supporting diversity. Actions such as these are only the beginning. Steps must be taken to help individuals identify their implicit and explicit biases and manage them. There must be an increased awareness of our stereotyping and microaggressions towards those who appear, speak or have different beliefs than ourselves. These efforts require a long-term commitment to overcome decades of misinformation and ignorance.

The American College Health Association (ACHA) notes, "Cultural competency is an engaging life-long journey of expanding your horizons, thinking critically about power and oppression and behaving appropriately."

REFERENCES

Juckett G. Caring for Latino Patients. *American Family Physician*. 2013; 87(1):48-54

Kumagai AK and Lypson ML. Beyond Cultural Competence: Critical Consciousness, Social Justice and Multicultural Education. *Academic Medicine*. 2009; 84(6): 782-787

Philips I and Tan C. Competence. *The Literary Encyclopedia*. https://courses.nus.edu.sg/course/elljwp/competence.htm

Tervalon M and Murray-Garcia J. Cultural Humility Verses Cultural Competence: A Critical Distinction in Defining Training Outcomes in Multicultural Education. *Journal of Health Care for the Poor and Underserved.*1998; 9: 117-125

CHAPTER 15

Understanding and Using a Multigenerational Workforce

Welcome diversity, develop skills and retain talent

The conclusion of each decade is accompanied by a new generation of individuals entering the workforce. Each group is tagged with a pluralistic term, e.g., generation X, Y, etc. Each group comes with its own set of expectations and aspirations. Each represents a new set of challenges and opportunities for leaders.

Let's start with the 55 and older segment of the workforce, "the Baby Boomers." They retain their position as the most significant senior leaders and managers across the corporate, entertainment, and political spectrum. Equally as important, according to the Department of Labor Statistics, in 2018, nearly half of all new jobs were taken by this group. An interesting array of factors contribute to this statistic. Older adult workers represent a source of proven, reliable, and skilled workers. They are a strong force despite the fact that members of this group are still retiring at a rate of nearly 10,000 per day. Those who remain or return to the workforce do so for a variety of reasons, including:

- They truly enjoy what they do. Their work serves as a source of great satisfaction and motivation for getting up every morning.
- It reaffirms their sense of self-worth and validates their ability to have a positive impact on the lives of others and play a role in the continued success of an organization.
- Many appreciate the opportunity to help others develop, to share their knowledge, and to watch the next generation become the leaders who ensure the stability of an organization.
- Some members of this older generation allocate a portion of their income to provide financial assistance to their adult children. They assist with a

down payment on a house, support extracurricular activities for grand-children, and contribute to a fund for their college education. They often view this as an expression of love, a privilege, and a source of joy.

- Simultaneously, many older adults have a haunting fear that there will not be enough in their nest egg to allow them to do all things on their "bucket list" or simply sustain them through their retirement years.

In contrast to the Baby Boomers, the 2016 Gallup Report "How Millennials Want to Work and Live" offers an in-depth look at this unique group in today's multigenerational workforce.

According to the Gallup report, the 80 million individuals born between 1980 and 1996, referred to as "millennials," represent the largest segment of the current workforce. Unlike their parents, they are much more adventurous. They are willing to challenge the status quo, are focused on work-life style balance, and are willing to explore other opportunities. Forty percent of millennials have college or advanced degrees. They represent the greatest proportion of the workforce with post-high school degrees.

Yet, according to a 2016 Gallup Report, they represent an interesting paradox. They have the highest percentage of employment (54%) but also the highest underemployed (10%) and unemployed (7%).

Engaged leaders will appreciate the following attributes of this group and seek to integrate them into a progressive workforce.

- Their command of digital technology would lead one to believe they began mastering these skills while still in the womb. They are social media masters with an iPad, iPhone, or iWatch that appear to be permanent appendages.
- They are incredibly adept in their ability to stay connected to everyone, anywhere, and with everything that matters to them. Such talent and skills are useful in developing a social media strategy for an organization.
- Perhaps the perception of wanting instant gratification and recognition might be more appropriately understood in other terms. They expect transparency, integrity, and honesty. They do want to know that their work, opinion, and insight are valued.
- While the potential for career advancement is desirable, as noted in the Gallup report, the satisfaction derived from the work they do is often more important than the money to be earned.

- They are capable of thinking beyond parochial needs. They tend to be more sensitive to all forms of inequities and disparities. More importantly, they are willing to try to rectify them.
- They view the informal work environment as the least important aspect of a job. Of greater significance is that their leaders/managers are clear about the job to be done and the priorities for achieving goals and objectives.
- Millennials' desire and need continuous feedback and effective communication.
- They want the opportunity to learn and grow. This is of paramount importance. They are willing to be accountable for their clearly defined responsibilities.

In addition to these attributes, there are a few other observations applicable to this group.

This fast-moving, fast-thinking generation wants instant gratification and recognition. It may be a reflection of their ability to be connected 24/7 rather than a pervasive aspect of how they function in the workplace. I am not convinced this is a universal characteristic of this group across all aspects of their lives. I have found this perception to be inconsistent with those who are parents and caregivers. They can be exceptionally patient, tolerant, and generous without expecting much in return. In addition, many are graduates of institutions requiring hours of community service which they continue as civic-minded individuals.

BENEFITS OF A MULTIGENERATIONAL WORKFORCE

- It enables an organization to attract and retain talented people of all ages.
- Teams can be more flexible and agile.
- Teams can meet the needs of a more diverse public and capture a greater share of the marketplace.
- Decisions are stronger because they are broad-based and reflect multiple perspectives.
- A multigenerational workforce can generate more innovative and creative ideas.

The challenge for today's leaders is to recognize the broad range of experience, skills, and aspirations of their workforce and blend them into a cohesive, productive organization. This may require an expansion of the leader's frame of reference, a reassessment of what he needs to get to where he wants to go and who he needs to help him get there.

WHERE ARE THESE MULTIGENERATIONS WORKING?

Leaders constantly pursue ways to be more efficient and cost-effective. Down time translates into lost revenue, failure to achieve goals and objectives, and failure to meet customer needs or expectations. In healthcare, this failure could have serious consequences for patients and caregivers. The need for guidance, consultation, and support is constant and often urgent. These services must be provided in a timely and accurate manner.

In today's world, meeting these multifaceted challenges means employing telecommunication, digital technology, and artificial intelligence. I have had first-hand experience with the capabilities of these technologies.

I recently had a telehealth visit with my doctor while sitting in my kitchen, attended a board of trustees meeting via WebEx, and had FaceTime with my grandchildren on an iPad. While visiting with my grandchildren in person, I had the joy of watching them go through their remote learning lessons in language arts, social studies, and math on Lexia and other digital programs. Perhaps one of the most recent entertaining experiences I've had was watching another family member play scrabble with the computer. There is little doubt that these technologies will continue to play a major role in every aspect of our lives and in the functional capabilities of organizations.

In the healthcare insurance industry, personnel who are capable of working remotely have become the norm. Health plan physicians and nurses who are involved in the prior approval process for hospital admissions and essential services must be accessible to doctors and patients at all times. Power failures, natural disasters, and widespread illness in a central office rarely mean that patients' needs go unmet.

Health plans have established special contingency operations to ensure that connectivity and essential services are maintained. These contingency plans include establishing telephone networks and practice shifting response capabilities from areas outages to those that have functional computer and communication services. Utility companies and educational systems employ similar actions in response to man-made or natural disasters.

The concept of working from home extends to all other aspects of the company's business. At my last leadership position, two-thirds of my department worked from home most of the time. When this capability was first offered, employees and managers were hesitant and had reservations about how this would work. Most of my staff were seasoned professionals who were accustomed to seeing their team members each day, interacting and collaborating in a tight-knit collegial manner. They shared knowledge and assisted each other. Yet, they wondered, "How is this work from home thing going to work?"

In a relatively short time, they began to appreciate the fact they were consummate professionals: competent, knowledgeable, and often self-directed. In addition, a quick consultation with a colleague was only an email, text message, or phone call away. Managers and supervisors also began to appreciate their continued capability to issue directives, monitor productivity, and meet established goals.

All that was left was for me, the leader, to adjust to was the idea that I was not leading a phantom department. I missed their smiles, hearing tidbits about families, and sharing the potluck lunches. When we were together, we had never missed an opportunity to celebrate something with a buffet of international delights.

Gradually, the concept of working remotely became an accepted reality for all of us. Quarterly meetings interspersed with expanded meetings that included members of other departments with whom we worked closely provided an opportunity to collaborate and share concerns with workflows or other day-to-day challenges. These sessions often yielded viable solutions or access to additional resources to improve operational efficiency. They also included educational presentations by staff and opportunities for informal conversations with personnel beyond individuals' respective departments.

One of the most significant outcomes of these meetings was a greater appreciation of the value that each person can contribute to the success of others. These meetings also helped some to understand their worth and to appreciate their potential to lead. All of these activities and experiences are important objectives of a transformational leader.

In addition to knowing the team members, the effective transformational leader must also prepare and equip them to function in a world of rapidly evolving technological innovations. Only a few decades ago, e-mails emerged as the new fast and easy way to communicate with multiple people while sitting at a desk. These transformations and many yet to be realized will continue to challenge the leaders of today and tomorrow.

Leaders of multigenerational, diverse workforces must be able to individualize their approaches to the members of this diverse workforce, engaging and motivating them by ensuring each has an opportunity to be heard, contribute, and develop. Although the trend of physical separation of team members is a reality, leaders can effectively maintain connectivity by utilizing the resources of technology.

REFERENCES

Gallup. How Millennials Want to Work and Live. Purpose. Development. Coach. Ongoing Conversations. Strengths. Life. The Six Big Changes Leaders Have to Make. Gallup.com. 2016.

Goler L, Gale J, Harrington B, and Grant A. Why People Really Quit Their Jobs. *Harvard Business Review.* July 11, 2018. https://hbr.org/2018/01/why-people-really-quit-their-jobs

Marston C. *Motivating The "What's in It for Me?" Workforce: Manage Across the Generational Divide and Increase Profits.* Hoboken, NJ: John Wiley & Sons; 2007.

Murphy SA. *Leading a Multigenerational Workforce.* Washington, DC: AARP; 2007.

Strecher VJ. *Life on Purpose: How Living for What Matters Most Changes Everything.* New York: Harper Collins; 2016.

Stacy S. *50 Nonclinical Careers for Physicians: Fulfilling, Meaningful and Lucrative Alternatives to Direct Patient Care.* Washington, D.C. American Association for Physician Leadership 2020.

Sisodia R, Wolfe D, and Sheth J. *Firms of Endearment: How World Class Companies Profit from Passion and Purpose.* Upper Saddle River, N.J.: Pearson Education; 2014.

Zweig D. Managing the "Invisibles." *Harvard Business Review.* May 2014. https://hbr.org/2014/05/managing-the-invisibles.

CHAPTER 16

The Gender Gap

Eliminate this gap now.

L eaders must reframe their thinking to reflect needed changes in the composition of a workforce. A prime area of focus should be on ensuring gender equality. Leaders' insight and sensitivity to these issues will guide their recognition of the necessity to change behaviors and modify an organization's culture.

To begin this re-framing their thinking, leaders must assess their subconscious biases, misconceptions, and culturally driven presumptions about women. In her book *Successful Women Think Differently*, Valerie Burton notes, "It is important to overcome thought patterns that sabotage success." Any leader who expects to transform his thinking and the culture of an organization must incorporate the intelligence, perspectives, and capabilities of women into the vision and strategic plan of an organization. Women's talents and skills cannot be ignored or inhibited; they must be fully supported and empowered as members of the leadership team.

Two major areas of concern regarding women in today's workforce are the gap in leadership and the gap in compensation.

GENDER GAP IN LEADERSHIP

Although some progress has been made in recent years, the gender gap in leadership for women is widespread. Men substantially outnumber women in leadership positions in business, education, military, and politics. This fact, however, does not reflect a lack of qualified candidates or educational preparation. Women:

- Comprise nearly 51% of the U.S. population and constitute
- 47% of the labor force. (Bureau of Labor Statistics)

- Earn approximately 60% of undergraduate degrees. (National Center for Education Statistics)
- Receive 60% of all master's degrees. (National Center for Education Statistics)
- Occupy almost 52% of all professional-level positions. (Bureau of Labor Statistics)

These data notwithstanding, women are significantly underrepresented in senior executive positions across all segments of the employment spectrum. In S&P 500 companies, women represent 44% of the workforce but only 25% of senior-level management. They occupy 20% of board seats and 2% of the CEO positions. In higher education, women comprise only 31% of full professors; only 27% of college presidents are women.

A woman's ability to lead has been well-established yet rarely fully appreciated or acknowledged. Queen Elizabeth II, Malala Yousafzai, and Michelle Obama each provide a unique perspective on women in leadership or influential positions in the 21st century.

Queen Elizabeth II is the longest-reigning monarch in the history of the British Commonwealth. Now in her nineties, she has committed her life to the service of the people in the commonwealth. Her extensive travels throughout the countries of the commonwealth and support of hundreds of charities, social and professional organizations have gained her the respect and admiration of millions of people and world leaders. The Queen is a constitutional monarch with three constitutional rights; the right to be consulted, to encourage, and to warn.

Queen Elizabeth II has skillfully employed these rights over more than six decades to effectively work with, advise and influence 12 prime ministers from Winston Churchill to Margaret Thatcher. Her actions qualify her as a transformational leader through her collaborations with these prime ministers through crises like the Suez Canal, Falkland Islands War, and the dissolution of 15 parliaments. She was also transformational by making the monarchy more transparent to the public by allowing access to coronations, weddings, and other royal activities.

Malala Yousafzai, from a different generation and culture, is a 24-year-old Pakistani woman, who at the age of 15, survived an assassination attempt because of her strong advocacy for the rights of women and children to be educated. After recovering from a gunshot wound to her head, Malala resumed her activist role for education with undaunted passion and devotion. Although she reigns over no one and leads no corporation, she has gained the love and respect of millions around the world for her leadership, courage, and commitment to educating women and children. In 2013 she was named one of *Time Magazine*'s most influential people. In 2014, she became the youngest person to be awarded the Noble Prize for Peace.

Michelle Obama, Princeton graduate, a prominent lawyer, was the first African American to serve as the First Lady of the United States. In 2008, she was named *Time Magazine*'s Woman of the Year. Two years after leaving the White House, she was named by *Good Housekeeping Magazine* as one of 120 Women Who Have Changed the World. Michelle Obama has achieved many notable accomplishments that have earned her these accolades. Four of the most notable are:

In 2010, she launched *Let's Move!*, bringing together community leaders, educators, medical professionals, parents, and others in a nationwide effort to address the challenge of childhood obesity.

In 2011, she and Dr. Jill Biden came together to launch *Joining Forces*, a nationwide initiative calling all Americans to rally around service members, veterans, and their families and support them through wellness, education, and employment opportunities.

In 2014, Mrs. Obama launched the *Reach Higher* Initiative, an effort to inspire young people across America to take charge of their future by completing their education past high school, whether at a professional training program, a community college, or a four-year college or university.

In 2015, Mrs. Obama joined President Obama to launch *Let Girls Learn*, a U.S. government-wide initiative to help girls around the world go to school and stay in school.

Although these women have achieved world prominence in distinctly different ways, at very different ages, they also have some common attributes that we associated with the best leaders and the **People Value Proposition**. They have committed their lives to improve the lives of others. They are pursuing their visions with unshakable determination, dignity, and integrity. They understand the importance of seeking value in others, acknowledge it, and help to enable that value to flourish.

To further illustrate the historical impact of women leaders, I offer the following examples of accomplished women.

Joan of Arc

The daughter of a tenant farmer in northwestern France, she never learned to read or write. However, the teachings of the Catholic Church were instilled in her. By the age of 13, she began to receive what she called "divine messages from God to save France." At the age of 18, she led the French army to defeat the English Burgundians at Orleans.

She was widely respected among French forces; however, some thought she was becoming too powerful and accused her of witchcraft, heresy, and dressing like a man. She was burned at the stake in 1431, at age 19, and canonized as a saint in 1920.

Harriet Tubman

Born into slavery in 1820 as Araminta Ross, she later adopted her mother's name, Harriet. In 1844, she married John Tubman, a free black man. Harriet worked as a maid, field hand, nurse, woodcutter, and as a scout and spy for the Union army during the Civil War. Her greatest accomplishment was as an abolitionist and leader of the Underground Railroad. Through the railroad, Harriet led hundreds of slaves to freedom.

Historian Thomas Wentworth Higgins referred to Harriet Tubman as "the greatest heroine of the age." The following quote by Harriet captures her tenacious spirit and determination, "There were one of two things I had a right to, liberty or death; if I could not have one, I would have the other; for no man should take me alive." She died in Auburn, New York, in 1913.

Frances Hesselbein

Hesselbein grew up in the mountains of western Pennsylvania. Following the death of her father, she dropped out of college after completing one semester to help care for her family. She went on to have a remarkable professional career, holding the position of president or CEO in four different companies. She often remarked that she had never applied for any of the positions and, in fact, had tried to refuse three of them.

Her last and most prominent position was as the CEO of the Girl Scouts of America. During her 13-year tenure, minority membership tripled, 250,000 new members were added, and the sale of cookies grew to over $300 million per year.

Peter Drucker, renowned author and management guru, described Hesselbein as "the best CEO in the US," noting, "She could manage any company in America." She died in 1915 at the age of 106.

Mary T. Barra

Born in 1961, Barra was 18 when she started working at General Motors. She earned a degree in electrical engineering from General Motors Institute (now Kettering University) and an MBA from Stanford University. She returned to GM and, over the next 15 years, began her ascent to the position of CEO of General Motors. In 2014, she became the first woman CEO to lead a major U.S. auto company.

Barra led GM to develop the Chevy Bolt EV, the first electric car for under $40,000, beating rival Tesla. She is known for her unique leadership style that utilizes her in-depth knowledge of the auto industry and cross-functional collaboration supported by three basic rules:

1. Keep it honest and keep it simple.
2. Make it about the company and the customer.
3. Use kinetic energy (their own energy) to mobilize people.

The women described in these examples, as well as countless others known and unknown embody many of the leadership qualities I have discussed in this book. Each embraces the principles of the People Value Proposition.

GENDER BIAS

Society has established numerous institutional and cultural barriers designed to exclude or diminish a woman's right to lead. These barriers are based on false assumptions about what a woman thinks, understands, needs, or is capable of doing.

If an employer has ever hesitated to hire a woman based on a concern for her commitment to her family, potential desire to have children, or ability to function under pressure, then explicit bias exists. The ethnicity of women can also influence hiring decisions even before they are in an organization.

I recall working with a White recruiter to hire a physician. My decision was to hire a Latina woman. The recruiter questioned the wisdom of my decision, given that I was African American in a predominantly White organization. I viewed this as a fairly blatant manifestation of racism embedded in the organization's culture. I ignored this concern and focused on the training and experience of the individual and knew that she would be an asset to my team. I hired her, and she proved to be a solid contributor to the medical staff.

I believe hiring practices based on unwritten or subtle rules may be carried out by men and women in hiring positions. These individuals are complicit in the bias of the institutional culture, perhaps because they are concerned about retribution from superiors. In the Mckinsey Report *Delivering on Diversity,* the data on the United States shows, "Women hold a disproportionately small share of line roles on executive teams, but women of color (including Black, Latina, and Asian) hold an even smaller share."

As the "Me Too" movement has gained public recognition, more women and men are stepping forward to acknowledge these concerns about gender abuse and intimidation. These gender concerns are now coupled with an intense focus on improving diversity, equity, and inclusion across all organizations and industries.

Gender bias is also manifested in the inability of some leaders to accept women as peers, meaningful contributors to the leadership team, and participants in strategic dialogue. For example, a woman who makes a statement similar to that of a male counterpart, with comparable tone and inflection, may be described as "bossy, aggressive, cold, emotional or opinionated" while the man is deemed "assertive, decisive, forceful."

Indeed, thought patterns, actions, and decisions that tend to minimize the role of women and negate their ability to provide leadership undermine the ultimate success of an organization. Thought patterns need to change, and definitive actions must be taken to change the perception about women's ability to lead.

There is hope. The *Missing Pieces Report:2018 Board Diversity Census of Women and Minorities on Fortune 500 Boards, a* multiyear study published by Deloitte and the Alliance for Board Diversity, found that 38.6 % of the Fortune 100's board seats and 34% of the Fortune 500's board seats are held by women and minorities. Both represent increases over 2016. At this rate, the percent of women and minorities on the respective boards could reach 40% by 2024.

Further analysis of the Fortune 500 seats gained by women between 2016 and 2018 reveals the following:

- White women continue to be the largest segment of women on the boards with an increase of 124 seats, up 13.9%.
- African-American women gained 32 seats, an increase of 28.2%.
- Asian/Pacific Islander women gained 17 seats, an increase of 38.6%.
- Hispanic/Latina women gained 4 seats, an increase of 9.8%.

The strongest correlation with diversity on these boards was the longevity of the company on the Fortune 500 hundred list. This suggests that the leaders of these organizations recognized the value that diversity could bring to their organizations; the organizations' longevity and profitability validate that vision.

A closer look at the Fortune 100 seats gained shows:

- The largest gains in 2018 were made by African-American and White women, with each gaining 13 seats, respectively.
- Asian/Pacific Islander women gained four seats.
- Hispanic/Latina women lost three seats.

The loss of seats by Hispanic/Latina women is not adequately explained in the report, given the importance of the Hispanic demographics and buying power in the U.S. Demographics (who you are, where you live, social-economic status) and buying power (ability to purchase a wide range of goods and services) are key drivers of marketing strategies for companies and are incentives for diverse workforces and governing boards.

The value of women in leadership roles is supported by research. A survey conducted by the Pew Research Center regarding women in business revealed that closing the gender gap would increase the global economy by nearly $28 trillion. Companies that committed to developing a gender-diverse executive leadership experienced 25% greater profitability. In addition, they were:

- 34% better at working out compromises.
- 34% more likely to be ethical and honest.
- 25 % more likely to stand up for their beliefs.

- 30 % more likely to provide fair pay.
- 25 % more effective at mentoring.

All of these attributes can contribute significantly to an organization's ability to retain the best employees and achieve greater productivity and profitability.

GENDER PAY GAP

The inequity of women's pay is nothing new. Before 1830, nearly all-American women worked from home. The 19th century Industrial Revolution created a critical need for an expanded workforce, and women stepped up to meet that need. Factories and mills in New England began hiring women who worked 14-hour days under deplorable conditions. In 1844, the first labor group was formed in Lowell, Massachusetts. The Lowell Female Labor Reform Association advocated for better working conditions and a 10-hour workday.

Conditions were far from ideal. Seventy percent of female immigrants arriving in New York City between 1880 and 1930 went to work in factories. Girls as young as eight years old and women as old as 60 worked long hours, for low pay, in unsafe conditions.

One of those individuals was Pauline Newman.

Born in Lithuania, she and her family immigrated to New York City in 1901. At the age of eight, Newman began working at the Triangle Shirtwaist Company, putting in 70-80 hours each week for $1.50 per week.

As a teenager, she gained a reputation as an avid activist for improving working conditions and higher pay. She was often at the center of planning strategies, leading strikes, and energizing crowds. In 1909, Newman quit her job at the Triangle factory and was appointed general organizer for the International Ladies Garment Workers Union (ILGWU). In this role, she traveled around the county organizing garment workers to achieve better working conditions and pay.

The battle for equal pay continued as women began to fill jobs usually occupied by men during World War II. In 1945, Congress proposed the Women's Equal Pay Act that stated women should be paid the same wage as men when performing the same job. Unfortunately, the measure failed to pass.

A renewed effort came during the administration of President John F. Kennedy when the Equal Pay Act of 1963 was passed as an amendment to the Fair Labor Standards Act of 1938. It was the first federal law to address gender discrimination. The Act mandated employers to pay equal wages and benefits to men and women performing the same job with the same skill, effort, and responsibility. It also included guidelines for when unequal pay was permitted, e.g., merit, seniority, quantity of production.

Significant progress has been made over the past five decades, but according to the 2018 Bureau of Labor Statistics, women 16 years of age and older working full-time are paid 81 cents compared to every dollar paid to men. This gap spans all occupations and extends across all 50 states for women working comparable jobs and hours per week. The question of why women are still paid less than men is yet to be answered or rectified.

Being aware of this historical perspective should incentivize leaders of today to act with a sense of urgency to end this legacy of inequality. Equal pay for equal work should be more than a slogan; it should be a reality championed by leaders of the 21st century. Leaders have a responsibility to promote, establish, and ensure women's access and equity in every organization.

REFERENCES

Burton V. *Successful Women Think Differently: 9 Habits to Make You Happier. Healthier & More Resilient*. Eugene, OR: Harvest House; 2012.

Rosen B. Leadership Journeys — Mary Barra: Harnessing Kinetic Energy at General Motors. IEDP Viewpoint. January 2014. www.iedp.com/articles/leadership-journeys-mary-barra.

Foster WZ. *The Negro People in American History*. New York: International Publishers; 1954.

Noland M and Moran T. Study: Firms with More Women in the C-Suite Are More Profitable. *Harvard Business Review*. February 2016. https://hbr.org/2016/02/study-firms-with-more-women-in-the-c-suite

Cohen WA. *Drucker on Leadership: New Lessons from the Father of Modern Management*. San Francisco: Jossey-Bass; 2010.

Alliance for Board Diversity. *Missing Pieces: The 2018 Board Diversity Census of Women and Minorities on Fortune 500 Boards*. ABD and Deloitte. 2019. www.catalyst.org/research/missing-pieces-report-the-2018-board-diversity-census-of-women-and-minorities-on-fortune-500-boards.

Horowitz JM, Igielnik R, and Parker K. *Women and Leadership 2018*. Pew Research Center. September 2018. www.pewresearch.org/social-trends/2018/09/20/women-and-leadership-2018/

SHRM. Fair Labor Standards Act of 1938. SHRM HR Public Policy Issues. www.shrm.org/hr-today/public-policy/hr-public-policy-issues/pages/fairlaborstandardsactof1938.aspx

U.S. Bureau of Labor Statistics. Highlights of Women's Earnings in 2018. BLS Reports. November 2019. www.bls.gov/opub/reports/womens-earnings/2018/home.htm

Hunt V, Prince S, and Dixon-Fyle S. *Delivering through Diversity*. London: McKinsey & Company; 2018.

Hunt V, Prince S, Dixon-Fyle S and Dolan K. *Diversity Wins: How Inclusion Matters*. London: McKinsey & Company; 2020.

Her Majesty the Queen. www.royal.uk/her-majesty-the-queen

The White House. First Lady Michelle Obama. https://obamawhitehouse.archives.gov/administration/first-lady-michelle-obama

Malala Yousafzai. Britannica. www.britannica.com/biography/Malala-Yousafzai

Ladd K. 120 Women Who Changed Our World. *Good Housekeeping*. March 2, 2108. https://www.goodhousekeeping.com/life/inspirational-stories/g2239/women-who-changed-our-world/?slide=14

Diversity and Inclusion: Social, Racial, Ethnic, Gender, and Religious Considerations

---

Diversity must be a strategic imperative viewed through a panoramic lens.

Diversity and inclusion are strong corollaries to culture and linguistic competence discussed earlier.

DIVERSITY

The U.S. Census Bureau projects that by 2050 the United States will no longer have a racial or ethnic majority. Diversity is a reality.

For leaders of organizations to remain competitive, excel, and lead in their respective marketplaces, they must not view the diversity of their workforce as a theoretical goal. Diversity must be a strategic imperative viewed through a panoramic lens. This will provide the broadest, most inclusive vision of diversity.

Gender, racial, LGBTQ, ethnic, and social diversity of the workforce must be major areas of focus, as should fully integrating religious beliefs and cultural traditions. To appreciate the broadest view of diversity, leaders must be aware of and prepare to include age, physical abilities, and special needs as additional elements of diversity. The commitment to become a diverse organization should begin immediately and should include the following objectives:

- All levels of leadership and management, as well as the workforce, should reflect the broadest spectrum of diversity.

- The organization's workforce should reflect the surrounding communities and countries in which it operates.
- Diversity goals should be clearly stated, achievable, reviewed, and modified if appropriate.
- Goals should have timelines; execution and achievement of goals must be assigned to accountable individuals.
- Human resource hiring practices must be consistent with diversity goals.
- The entire organization should have ongoing training conducted by experts in the field to reinforce diversity goals.
- Leaders of organizations should seek referrals from their current diverse employees as well as leaders and members of diverse community organizations.

Leaders who embrace diversity as a strategic imperative for their organization will strive to actively recruit and hire people with different experiences, perspectives, and functional backgrounds. Historian Doris Kearns Goodwin wrote in her book *Leadership in Turbulent Times,* "Good leadership requires you to surround yourself with people of diverse perspectives who can disagree with you without fear of retaliation."

INCLUSION

Inclusion is the key to making diversity a reality. Inclusion of the most diverse workforce unequivocally signals an organization's commitment to diversity. Inclusion must be an integral part of the organization's culture and can only be validated through its visible presence, not through proclamation. The culture of organizations and their leaders must embrace the tenets of diversity and inclusion to adapt to the changes in the composition of today's workforce.

Inclusion is realized when the engagement of all employees is a priority. This may mean communicating the same message in different ways to different segments of the workforce. Inclusion means that everyone has an opportunity to participate and contribute. Leaders must be aware of their preconceived notions of an individual, their implicit or explicit biases that inhibit the participation or contribution of the individual. Leaders' lack of awareness or inability to manage these deficits contribute directly to the exclusion, not inclusion, of individuals.

These important steps can foster inclusion:

1. Encourage senior executives to sponsor affinity groups for employees focused on promoting ethnic, racial, and religious understanding; celebrating cultural, gender, ethnic, and religious identities; and serving as mentors.
2. Include diversity and inclusion training in the orientation of new employees.
3. Enable everyone to participate or contribute.
4. Do not allow "the loudest voice" to dominate a meeting or exclude the voices of others.
5. Create opportunities for the education and sharing of religious, ethnic, cultural, and other traditions with the entire workforce.
6. Recognize the need for flexibility of schedules to observe and accommodate certain religious or cultural beliefs and customs.
7. Ensure that everyone has equal access to career development, acquisition of skills, and education opportunities.
8. Create opportunities for team members to meet and collaborate with colleagues from other departments on all issues that require a collective effort to deliver the best results.
9. Promote or require the participation and inclusion of all individuals or groups.
10. Work to eliminate a "silo mentality" with individuals and departments.

THE BUSINESS CASE FOR DIVERSITY AND INCLUSION

Josh Bersin, the founder of the Josh Bersin Academy, an organization that helps human resource entities address business and talent issues, clearly states the case: "Companies that embrace diversity and inclusion in all aspects of their business statistically outperform their peers."

In the May 2020 report, *Diversity Wins: How Inclusion Matters,* McKinsey & Company describe how four major corporations have taken aggressive action to strengthen the business case for diversity and inclusion. Citigroup, Pentair, Target, and Lockheed Martin have all committed to programs to enhance equity, be more open to ways to eliminate barriers that have inhibited the development of more diverse and inclusive cultures. It is acknowledged that while the business case is stronger, the overall progress is slow. Executive teams with more than 30% women are more likely to financially outperform those with fewer or no women by 25 to 48%.

Leaders of today's organizations should implement a diverse and inclusive culture with a deliberate sense of urgency. This pursuit is important enough to incorporate it into the mission.

- **Greater Revenue Streams.** The Boston Consulting Group reported in 2017 that organizations with above-average diversity scores created 19% greater revenue streams from innovations than organizations with below-average diversity scores.
- **Greater Profitability.** In the *Delivering Through Diversity* report by McKinsey Consultants, companies that committed to developing a gender-diverse executive leadership experienced a 25% greater profitability. In addition, companies that were in the top quartile for cultural and ethnic diversity had a 33% increase in profitability.

The benefits to organizations that do this well are well-documented and indicative of a highly engaged workforce. Research shows that an engaged workforce — one that is *inclusive* — leads to:

- **Increased Earnings per Market Share.** Companies with high levels of engagement have earnings per share that are 2.6 times higher than companies with low engagement scores.
- **Lower Turnover.** Companies in the bottom quartile of engagement have a 41% higher turnover rate.
- **Higher Net Income.** Companies with high engagement scores have net income that is two times higher than companies with low engagement scores.
- **Increased Profitability.** The Corporate Leadership Council indicates that companies with highly engaged employees generated profits nearly three times faster than competitors.
- **Increased Growth.** A MacLeod & Clarke study in the United Kingdom showed companies with highly engaged workforces experienced an average 19.2% growth over a 12-month period.

SOCIAL DIVERSITY

The diverse populations in metropolitan areas throughout the United States have frequently been referred to as "melting pots." The term is a misnomer in that it implies that the people in these cities have blended into this amorphous mass called "Americans." While it is true that they are proud to be Americans, there is ample evidence that they also are determined to retain their ethnic, social, cultural, and religious heritage and traditions.

It is common to find ethnic, cultural, or social communities like Little Italy, Chinatown, or Little Haiti in metropolitan cities throughout the United States. St. Patrick's Day, Columbus Day, Caribbean Day, Gay Pride Day, and Puerto Rican Day parades are only a few of the many expressions of ethnic, social, and cultural diversity. These events are viewed by thousands of spectators who share in the joy and beauty of various cultural identities. Observances such as Chanukah, Diwali, Ramadan, and Kwanza have become an integral part of American society. The people participating in these activities expect their cultures and traditions to be recognized and respected in their communities and in the workplace.

Katherine Phillips, distinguished professor at the Kellogg School of Management at Northwestern University and the Columbia Business School, acknowledges that social diversity can trigger discomfort, distrust, interpersonal conflict, disrespect, diminished communication, and lack of cohesion. Phillips notes that extensive research by organizational scientists, psychologists, sociologists, and others has clearly established that social diversity is not just a desired asset. In fact, social diversity is a necessity for those organizations that want to inspire creativity and innovation, encourage and develop new perspectives, and foster better decision-making and problem-solving.

Employees from each generation of diverse cultures and backgrounds want to be meaningful contributors to their companies, to be included and not subject to disparities and inequities. It is incumbent upon every leader to acknowledge and, when possible, celebrate the social diversity of a workforce.

RELIGIOUS BELIEFS AND CULTURAL TRADITIONS

People's religious beliefs and traditions are often reflected in what they wear, whether it is a yarmulke, hijab, or turban. These items of clothing can trigger a set of assumptions about these individuals, including assumptions about their ability to do a job, be valued members of a team, or lead. These assumptions are manifestations of religious intolerance.

Leaders are responsible for recognizing and respecting these differences and taking specific steps to change behaviors and enhance the culture of an organization. These steps may include:

- Mandate that all senior leaders and managers respect these differences as reflected in their hiring, mentoring, and employee career development practices.
- Ensure that all hiring practices adhere to job requirements and are not influenced by a candidate's religious or cultural differences.
- Provide program opportunities for religious and cultural groups to share information and educate the entire workforce.
- Facilitate the formation of affinity groups with corporate officer sponsors to demonstrate the support and commitment to these groups.
- Develop cafeteria menus that accommodate the dietary restrictions and traditional meals of the different groups.
- Ensure tolerance of hair styles (cornrows, dreadlocks, various color streaks, or dyes).
- Manage staffing requirements to accommodate religious or other culturally significant holidays/events.

RACIAL AND ETHNIC PERCEPTIONS

In her paper *Diversity Leadership: Influence of Ethnicity, Gender and Minority Status*, Jean L. Chin notes, "Conceptualizations of leadership need to be inclusive of the social identities and lived experiences that leaders and followers both bring to the contexts of leadership."

Social identities are the functional units of a pluralistic, socially diverse society. They include the racial identities and ethnic origins of individuals. They can have a greater impact on first impressions than appearance.

I found this to be true on one occasion when I accompanied my wife to a social event related to her work. I was dressed in a suit and tie and found myself standing alone in the middle of a room while my wife was conversing with some associates. I was approached by a white-haired Caucasian man dressed in a pair of slacks, V-neck sweater shirt, and tie. In a somewhat sarcastic tone, he asked, "Who are you, standing in the middle of the floor trying to look so important?"

Several caustic rejoinders raced through my mind, but I held my tongue, not wanting to create an incident that might reflect badly on my wife. I simply answered, "No one, just waiting for my wife." I later learned this gentleman considered himself a local political power broker.

This was not my first encounter with a narrow type of thinking.

I experienced a similar incident when I was a medical student. During one of my clinical rotations, I was walking down a corridor, wearing a white jacket with a stethoscope slung around my neck. As I approached an area of vendor machines, a woman, red-faced, fuming with frustration in front of an ice cream machine, turned to me and blurted out," I'm so glad you're here, this machine has taken my money and not given me my ice cream." That she thought I was there to fix the machine was initially somewhat amusing. Then, it occurred to me to ask myself whether her reaction would have been the same if she had seen one of my Caucasian colleagues wearing a white coat and carrying a stethoscope.

How I appeared through the eyes and minds of others frequently negated who I was and what value I could contribute. Unfortunately, this social identity based on my racial identity has continued to be a recurring experience throughout my life. But these experiences have served me well. They have enabled me to persevere through many adversities, each one forcing me to remember who I am and not who others perceive me to be.

These racial, ethnic, religious, and gender identity experiences also remind me that far more people saw value in me than did not. Most important, they strengthen my resolve to always seek the value that anyone may have and to judge them by what they do, not on how they appear or their cultural or social background.

Leaders must avoid making assumptions based on an individual's race, gender, physical ability, sexual orientation, or religion. They must redefine their thinking so that it is not encumbered by presumptions about what one "can bring to the table" before they have even been invited to have a seat.

The following areas are often influenced by how one perceives race and ethnicity.

Assertive Versus Hostile

An individual's contribution to a discussion may well depend on the speaker's gender, racial, ethnic, or religious background. I have witnessed discussions in which a White male who makes a strong declarative statement is described as "assertive" or "having a command presence." A person of color who speaks emphatically or assertively may be described as "hostile," "belligerent," "pushy," or simply dismissed. This reaction reflects one's intrinsic or subconscious bias, exclusionary attitude, or tendency to apply stereotypes.

Posing Questions Versus Obstructionist

When some individuals ask questions, they are considered thoughtful and appropriate. Others, often those of particular racial, ethnic, or religious backgrounds, who ask the same questions are deemed obstructionists who are delaying the flow of a meeting or impeding progress toward a goal.

VARIOUS POINTS OF VIEW VERSUS RESISTANCE

As was the case with those asking questions, a different point of view offered by those in leadership positions is seen as insightful or refreshing. The opinion of people in subordinate roles may be seen as unworthy, insignificant, or resistant to change. When these opinions are regularly dismissed or ignored, it conveys a message that one's perspective has little value, that constructive criticism is not tolerated, and the experience behind an opinion is not appreciated.

LISTENING TO THE MESSAGE VERSUS LISTENING TO THE PERSON

In earlier chapters, I emphasized the importance of a leader being able to listen, which is the key to being able to engage, motivate, and lead. A leader's failure to listen to an employee undermines that leader's ability to build an effective line of communication. It also diminishes a leader's opportunity to provide clarity, empathy, and respect. This view is based on personal experience.

At times, I believed that certain leaders ignored my remarks. This reaction raised serious concerns, especially when a more senior person spoke after me, essentially reiterating my comments, and was recognized as saying something noteworthy.

If my comments were unclear or confusing, developing more effective communication skills would have been a good topic for an individual feedback or coaching session. Anyone who leads, manages, or supervises employees has a primary responsibility to help each individual become the best he or she can be. This includes helping employees to improve their communication skills. Effective communication skills must be viewed as a critical component to successfully executing responsibilities and relating to colleagues and customers.

SEEING THE BIG PICTURE VERSUS INABILITY TO FOCUS

When an individual can think and see beyond the scope of a current discussion, she may be described as a visionary or strategic thinker. She can anticipate potential events or unintended consequences and initiate actions to address them.

On the other hand, someone else can make similar observations and be labeled as being out of touch or unable to focus on the business at hand. This is certainly possible, but when that person has established himself as a competent, knowledgeable individual, the label signals a lack of respect or perceived threat to a leader's position of authority.

Leaders need to be sensitive to these scenarios for themselves and their team members. These inappropriate responses dampen motivation and impede innovative or creative thinking. They essentially negate an opportunity to assess and develop the next generation of executive leadership, as well as to nurture a collegial atmosphere where everyone is respected and opinions valued.

BIAS AND INTOLERANCE

Implicit bias

We all have preferences in the food we eat, the music we listen to, or the books we like to read. These are biases we can easily identify. It is far more difficult to discern those spontaneous thoughts or reactions that result in presumptions about an individual's capabilities or ability to make meaningful contributions. These presumptions are the foundation of implicit bias, the barrier to an inclusive and diverse organizational culture.

Once implicit bias is acknowledged, taking action to understand and overcome it requires introspection and an unwavering commitment to become more inclusive. This will require a long-term commitment to open, honest discussions about complex issues, as Emmanuel Acho presents in his book, *Uncomfortable Conversations with a Black Man.* Acho offers a four-step approach to address these issues:

1. *No Question Is Off-limits.* For example, "What are some of the ways to find and get rid of your implicit bias?
2. *Let's Rewind.* Look for the historical influences, root causes, and published research to understand the origin, if possible, of an issue.
3. *Let's Get Uncomfortable.* Each participant must engage in an open, honest discussion about what the issue means to him and what might be done to alter perceptions or beliefs.
4. *Talk it, Walk it.* Each person must then develop his own plan to change and remain committed to it. It cannot be a "one size fits all" approach for individuals or organizations.

Inclusivity in the workplace cannot be achieved by simply holding an annual diversity training exercise. The effort must begin with leaders and managers and be manifested in every way, every day, by everyone. The guiding principles must be clear, communicated to everyone, and consistently practiced. These principles allow everyone the opportunity to be heard, to be connected, and to contribute.

Leaders must recognize the advantages of the social identities of those they lead, make every effort to include them, and be prepared to manage the shortcomings of each. It is important to realize there is no single approach or perspective that will meet everyone's needs. Our goal is to set the example that the succeeding generation will embrace and strive to improve.

Leaders and followers are composites of their life experiences. Each will be influenced by the past, but the ability to move forward requires leaders, managers, and all team members to be open to new people, new ideas, and new experiences. Become a "bias interrupter," as Joan C. Williams recommends in her *Harvard Business Review* article, "How the Best Bosses Interrupt Bias on Their Team."

The following describe guiding principles to be a "bias buster":

- Apply the same set of criteria for core competencies, expected behaviors, and respect to everyone.
- Insist on diversity at every level of an organization, from board members and executive leaders to custodians.
- Give everyone an opportunity to learn, develop, and lead meaningful projects.
- Allow everyone to express an opinion or offer a perspective in meetings.
- Avoid making assumptions or judgments based on racial or ethnic stereotypes, gender, religious or sexual orientation.
- Give credit or acknowledge the value of something said or done to the person who initiated it, not to the higher-ranking person who repeats it.
- Incorporate these principles, on a daily basis, into the way you supervise, manage, direct, or lead.

To be a successful bias buster, a leader must first acknowledge that bias exists in its numerous manifestations. The leader must believe it is possible to change the status quo. The leader must articulate the benefits of eliminating bias and then rigorously apply the guiding principles to do so.

RETAIN THE BEST, DISCARD THE REST?

The most competent, respected, effective leaders are those who surround themselves with the most knowledgeable and skilled people they can find. Finding them involves listening, engaging, and challenging potential team members to identify the best.

The leader who believes that his or her opinion, vision, or perception is the best and is all that matters will inevitably fail to achieve, let alone exceed optimal success. These leaders have no desire to lead. They surround themselves with those who reinforce their thinking, ignore suggestions to improve or enhance the vision or achieve the promise of the mission. Those who cannot comply with this expectation are soon discarded.

"Discarding the rest" means not nurturing creative new talent, not appreciating experienced, insightful individuals. They are not given an opportunity to enrich this leader's experience or enhance his ability to deliver on the promises made or to deliver better than expected results.

Thus, to avoid the loss of valuable personnel, a leader must thoroughly assess the skills and assets of a potential team member before making the decision to discard.

Leaders must take the time to engage and listen to people who do not meet a preconceived or traditional image. They must look for the value in people who appear less than ideal but who can contribute substantially to the success of the team. The most effective leaders insist on mutual respect, trust, and integrity to serve as the pillars to support efficient teamwork that delivers reliable results. Leaders must set the example that enables their teams to embrace these pillars as core competencies. This leadership must be demonstrated not just in town hall meetings, memos, or posters, but in actions.

In addition, leaders must make every effort to combat an organizational culture infused with all forms of bias. Explicit, implicit, or unconscious bias and a judgmental attitude do not convey a culture of mutual respect and equal opportunity. Deliberate exclusion or avoidance are not incentives for employees to be loyal or to believe there is a viable future in such a culture.

Any training program designed to develop a commitment to diversity and inclusion and address implicit, explicit, or subconscious bias must focus on rectifying the gap in gender leadership and pay. These critical steps will create an organization that is not only culturally competent but also optimally functional.

REFERENCES

Acho E. *Uncomfortable Conversations with a Black Man*. New York: Flatiron Books; 2020.

Chin JL. Diversity Leadership: Influences of Ethnicity, Gender and Minority Status. *Open Journal of Leadership*. 2013; 2(1):1-10.

Dubey R. and Hirsch AS. Viewpoint: Building a Business Case for Diversity and Inclusion. SHRM. March 19, 2018. www.shrm.org/resourcesandtools/hr-topics/behavioral-competencies/global-and-cultural-effectiveness/pages/viewpoint-building-a-business-case-for-diversity-and-inclusion.aspx

Ehman J. Religious Diversity: Practical Points for Health Care Providers. Penn Medicine. April 2007. www.uphs.upenn.edu/pastoral/resed/diversity_points.html

Eswaran V. The Business Case for Diversity in the Workplace Is Now Overwhelming. World Economic Forum. April 29, 2019. www.weforum.org/agenda/2019/04/business-case-for-diversity-in-the-workplace.

Goodwin J. Amazon Adds More Executive Diversity with the Appointment of First Black Woman to Its Senior Leadership Team. CNN Business. August 25, 2020. www.cnn.com/2020/08/25/tech/amazon-first-black-executive-senior-leadership-team-bezos/index.html

Hunt V, Prince S, Dixon-Fyle S. *Delivering through Diversity*. London: McKinsey & Company; 2018.

Jarrett E. Diversity Is More Than Just the Kind You Can See. TLNT blog. September 20, 2018. www.tlnt.com/the-many-types-of-diversity-should-be-on-your-teams/#:~:text=Diversity%20of%20opinion%2C%20outlook%20and,hire%20people%20similar%20to%20themselves.

Kerns Goodwin D. *Leadership in Turbulent Times*. New York: Simon and Schuster; 2018.

Kosoff M. Amazon Has a White Man Problem: Beyond Social Justice, Experts Call It a Business Liability. OneZero. February 27, 2019. https://onezero.medium.com/amazon-has-a-white-man-problem-179e9759f35b

Noland M, and Moran T. Study: Firms with More Women in the C-Suite Are More Profitable. *Harvard Business Review*. February 8, 2016. https://hbr.org/2016/02/study-firms-with-more-women-in-the-c-suite-are-more-profitable

Phillips KW. How Diversity Makes Us Smarter. Scientific American. Octobeer 2104. https://www.scientificamerican.com/article/how-diversity-makes-us-smarter.

Pinkett R, Robinson J, and Patterson P. *Black Faces in White Places: 10 Game-Changing Strategies to Achieve Success and Find Greatness*. New York: AMACOM; 2011.

Staples B. How Italians Became White. *The New York Times*. October 12, 2019. https://www.nytimes.com/interactive/2019/10/12/opinion/columbus

CHAPTER 18

Perpetual Cycle of Leadership

An outstanding leader establishes a legacy of
success and develops a team to sustain it

A ll organizations have a code of conduct. For some organizations, it is well defined in writing and reinforced annually through required training. For other organizations, the code of conduct is more informal and simply stated: "it's the way we do business." Like the training in the medical profession discussed in the **"See One, Do One, Teach One"** section, the ability of a workforce to follow directions, work effectively with others, and execute a strategy is dependent on all levels of leadership in the organization. Thus, the continuous development of leaders is crucial.

A leader's legacy isn't measured solely by an organization's financial strength, position in the marketplace, or recognition received. Rather, visionary leaders must also ensure that their successors are prepared to assume increasing responsibility, meet new challenges, and sustain the success achieved. That preparation should include several key attributes.

The next generation of leaders will be confident, committed, and connected with those they lead.

A CONFIDENT LEADER

The confident leader remains focused in the presence of extreme pressure and acts with a sense of urgency guided by a thoughtful assessment of the big picture. A leader who displays confidence reassures the members of his team. He conveys direction and a rationale for their actions. Incorporated in the rationale are a clear vision, adherence to core values, and an appreciation of the capabilities of the team.

The leader is able to think strategically while simultaneously empowering others to align people and resources to execute the strategy. By empowering his team members, he conveys trust in their ability to assume responsibility, be accountable, and lead.

A COMMITTED LEADER

A committed leader leads not only with integrity but also with the determination to exhibit behaviors that demonstrate consistent pride and competence in their work. She consistently practices and promotes the principles of cultural humility and linguistic and cultural competence. She rejects being ordinary; she continuously strives to be exceptional.

The committed leader knows that it is not just the number of hours devoted to work but also the quality of products produced, services delivered, staff developed, and satisfied customers or clients helped during those hours. This is equally applicable to those engaged in nonprofit endeavors as it is for global corporations.

The committed leader encourages team members to exhibit behaviors that demonstrate consistent, core competencies in whatever work they do, the service they provide, or product they produce.

A CONNECTED LEADER

A connected leader engages employees in any setting. He communicates in clear decisive terms and recognizes when reassurance and guidance are needed. He understands the importance of a collaborative effort at all levels of an organization and discourages a "silo-centric mentality" (those who only want to work within their own sphere of influence) but ensures appropriate recognition of accomplishments.

A connected leader appreciates the importance of work-life balance and strives to create an organization in which neither is sacrificed. The connected leader recognizes the necessity to redefine the organization's culture to adapt to changes in political, social, and regulatory environments.

The confident, committed, and connected leader knows that his tenure as a leader is limited. The leader who truly cares about the organization and people he leads wants them to continue to succeed after he moves on. This commitment to ensuring continued growth evokes an implied responsibility to incorporate leadership development as an essential component of an organization's culture.

The confident, committed, and connected leader defines the direction for an organization and builds a cohesive team to chart the course. The leader provides opportunities that motivate and inspire and develops a continuous cadre of leaders.

THE PERPETUAL CYCLE OF LEADERSHIP

The perpetual cycle of leadership embodies the adage of **See One, Do One, Teach One**. In my view, this tenet dispels the notion that one is born to be a doctor, nurse, caregiver, or leader.

In the introduction of this book, I noted that 86% of organizations surveyed by Deloitte are not comfortable with their development of leadership. While each of us may possess certain innate characteristics that enable us to excel, the development of the total leadership skill set requires training, guidance, and knowledge, coupled with the opportunity for development and practical experience.

The perpetual cycle of leadership requires a leader to understand the importance of instilling in those he has led, the need to perpetuate the qualities of effective leadership.

The next generation of leaders must appreciate the current measures of success but be committed to improving that which can be better. When they assume the responsibility of leading, they mark the beginning of a new legacy and the perpetuation of the cycle of leaders.

REFERENCES

Colmen D. *12 Choices That Lead to Your Success*. Dallas, TX: Cornerstone Leadership Institute; 2005.

Gallup. How Millennials Want to Work and Live. Gallup. 2016. https://enviableworkplace.com/wp-content/uploads/Gallup-How-Millennials-Want-To-Work.pdf.

Hougaard R. The Real Crisis in Leadership. *Forbes*. September 9, 2018.

Moldoveanu M and Narayandas D. The Future of Leadership Development. *Harvard Business Review*. March 2019. https://hbr.org/2019/03/the-future-of-leadership-development

Swartz J and Peister B. Human Capital Trends 2014 Survey. Deloitte. 2014. www2.deloitte.com/us/en/insights/focus/human-capital-trends/2014/human-capital-trends-2014.

CHAPTER 19

I Can

---

*A visionary leader sees the promise of
tomorrow and pursues it today*

"**I** CAN" is an acronym that captures the essence of the concepts explored in the preceding chapters. These concepts represent a code of conduct or set of core competencies for leaders. They redefine the scope of leadership, describe who can lead, and delineate when to lead.

I am not aware of anything in the study of the human genome that has revealed a gene for leadership. Thus, I place little emphasis on the thought that individuals are born to lead. The elements in "I CAN" represent a primer on how to nurture and develop leadership.

I — INSPIRE INNOVATION

As a leader, I must continuously strive to inspire others through my own actions and behavior. I must act with integrity.

When I can motivate others to be inspired, I am facilitating their potential for innovative or creative thinking.

I will insist on the best effort. If that effort fails to yield the desired results, I will use it as a teachable moment. I will view it as an opportunity to reassess a strategic initiative, highlight the awareness of variables that may influence the issue, or redefine a plan of action.

To nurture in this culture means to neutralize negativity that can be manifested in many ways.

I will act to rectify an error or identify an alternate approach, rather than deflecting the responsibility or blame to someone else. I will use these instances as opportunities for crafting constructive criticism, building confidence, and providing a new perspective.

I will be timely in voicing disagreement or dissatisfaction with an action or behavior.

C — COMMUNICATE

I will never take my ability to communicate for granted. I will be aware and monitor my tone, inflection, and body language constantly. I will recognize that they may often have a greater impact on my audience than my words.

I will be sensitive to the fact that a failure to appreciate the intellectual maturity, professional insight, and expected social etiquette of those I lead can be viewed as a sign of disrespect. In turn, this can result in a disconnect and ineffective communication.

I will also recognize the need to provide a rationale for taking a particular action. I acknowledge this important element will enable a team to move forward with confidence and purpose in executing a directive.

I will make an earnest effort to connect with those I lead in a genuine and direct manner. I will use phone calls, e-mails, and text messages as needed, but I will seize every opportunity to connect with anyone directly.

Whenever possible, I will send a hand-written note or card to convey a special thank you or express appreciation.

Despite all the advantages we enjoy in this age of digital technology, a smile, a kind word, and a helping hand will remain my gold standard for connecting with people. It is an easy and inexpensive standard to maintain.

I will make a lifetime commitment to adhere to this gold standard, to apply it every day, to everyone, anywhere. I will not ignore the use of digital technology. Rather, I pledge to use my interpersonal skills daily and employ digital technology appropriately.

I acknowledge that communicating and connecting electronically has become an essential capability, not a luxury. It has become the primary mechanism, not only for communicating the same message to many people, but also for educating, tracking progress, and reinforcing compliance.

I will strive to be technologically competent and committed to personal connections whenever possible.

A — ACCOUNTABLE

I will accept responsibility for an action or error. I will identify the root cause and take appropriate steps to correct or rectify mistakes.

I will acknowledge that an appropriate correction may require the insight and perspective that exceed my capabilities. I will actively seek the counsel of those with proven expertise to enhance the accuracy of my decision-making.

I will do my homework to learn about and comprehend the dimensions of the issue I am confronting.

I will listen to different perspectives. Listening will enable me to reach informed, appropriate decisions. Listening may also facilitate my acceptance of an approach that was beyond my original vision.

My acceptance of a new approach will enable me to appreciate the value, diversity, knowledge, and experience of those I lead.

When I demonstrate the ability to accept different views, I reassure those I lead that they can believe in me. Those who would follow my lead must be convinced not only of the principles I espouse but also how well I adhere to them.

I can instill confidence in my leadership by reassuring them of the value that each contributes.

I can ensure respect, trust, and loyalty by assuring that promises made are promises kept.

N — NURTURE

I can do something to foster the growth and development of anything beyond myself; I can nurture a plant, a child, or a fellow employee. In each case, I can acknowledge the value within and seek to enhance it. In doing so, my efforts will rarely go unrewarded.

I will strive to demonstrate the hallmarks of a capable leader; the provision of guidance, the sharing of knowledge, and the offering of insights to fellow employees.

I recognize that the strength of a team is defined by the collective capabilities of each member. The ability to succeed at any task is based on the value of the individuals engaged in the effort.

I must accept nurturing as a long-term commitment. For people, nurturing can be in the form of encouragement, motivation, and an opportunity for development. In turn, this stimulates inspiration and innovation. The nutrients are the access to knowledge, training, and the acquisition of new skills.

I understand that people who benefit from the nurturing invested will often seek new opportunities for advancement within their existing organization. I will make every effort to create appropriate opportunities for advancement. I will be aware of the value of individuals and take appropriate action to facilitate their growth and retention. However, I also realize there will be those who will seek opportunities outside of the organization.

While it is always an objective to retain the best employees, it is not always possible to do so. When I appreciate the true value of an employee, I want that individual to be in a setting that most effectively accommodates her passion, desire for advancement and can be compensated appropriately. If I feel I have done everything possible to retain this individual, her departure is an experience of both regret and pride. I want her to succeed wherever she goes.

I must work to establish a culture that goes beyond the fundamentals of good management. The culture must exceed the basic expectations of the employee who wants to stay in an organization. This employee seeks an ongoing dialogue that goes beyond semi-annual reviews with a supervisor, manager, or director. This employee wants to feel like an integral part of the team, not an expendable appendage.

I will nurture this culture by neutralizing negativity and focusing on positive reinforcement. Rather than belittle, embarrass, or humiliate, I will seek to illuminate the source of an error, educate, and motivate.

I will act to rectify an error or identify an alternative approach rather than deflecting the blame or responsibility to someone else. I will use such instances as opportunities for crafting constructive criticism, building confidence, or providing a new perspective.

I will be timely in voicing disagreement or dissatisfaction with an action or behavior and move with a sense of urgency to provide a clear rationale for a position or definitive corrective action.

As a nurturing leader:

- I will ensure that seeking value in others is the norm.
- I will consider everyone to be significant, every perspective worthy of consideration and every insight to have potential value.
- I will work to perpetuate a culture that thrives on the belief that everyone matters. Every job and responsibility is an integral piece of sustainable success.
- I will express an alternative view or articulate current expectations in a manner that conveys confidence and reassurance.
- I will practice cultural humility and facilitate diversity and inclusion in every way possible.
- Being a leader should not be about what I do to make me great, but rather what I do to make others better.

If I exhibit this behavior, act with integrity and seek the value in myself that I expect of others, the value of what we do will be apparent and will be manifested in success.

CHAPTER 20

Reflections on Leadership in a Challenging Time

In Spring 2020, nearly 14 years after I completed my master's degree in organizational communication and leadership, my concept of leadership and my perception of those who lead and those who have the potential to lead was tested by some of the most difficult challenges our nation and the world has faced in my lifetime.

The lives of people all over the world were disrupted by the COVID-19 global pandemic. The devastating impact of the virus on the health of millions of Americans was just beginning. This devastation was accompanied by an equally crushing impact on both the economy and education systems. One of the most significant factors contributing to the catastrophic toll of COVID-19 was the failure of leadership at multiple levels.

In May 2020, life was slowly pressed out of the body of George Floyd, a Black man in Minneapolis. The event triggered a Black Lives Matter outcry that reverberated in cities throughout the U.S. and around the world. The incident galvanized a large, diverse array of citizens, all committed to ending social injustice and systemic racism. The protests continued for months, marred by those who saw it as an opportunity to burn and loot stores, exercise an inappropriate use of force on demonstrators, assault law enforcement personnel, and incite violence to undermine the peaceful intent of the civil actions.

To further test the will and fortitude of Americans, residents of the west coast watched raging fires consume millions of acres, destroying hundreds of homes and causing the deaths of too many.

Meanwhile, a concomitant crisis was occurring in the southern gulf states as they were hammered by one hurricane after another. The powerful winds and flood waters devastated many towns and homes.

As Fall 2020 approached, we were bombarded with a relentless flood of political sound bites and infinite analyses, speculation, and in some instances, misinformation about the upcoming presidential election. Each day, the political rhetoric grew more vile and more divisive. Nevertheless, we were expected to make intelligent, informed decisions. The need for leaders who embrace the tenets of the People Value Proposition was never more critical.

In the following discussion, I will highlight some of the key aspects and consequences of the COVID-19 pandemic and the challenges of social injustice and systemic racism, and where our leaders have embraced and rejected the tenets of the People Value Proposition.

THE COVID-19 CRISIS

In the summer of 2020, the people of the United States constituted 4.25% of the world's population but accounted for nearly 20% of all deaths from COVID-19. As I write this, the number of reported cases in the United States has passed 10 million; more than a quarter of a million American lives have been lost to COVID-19.

Multiple factors have contributed to these tragic numbers. Little was known about the nature of this virus at the onset; hospital systems lacked necessary critical care space and beds for those who needed to be hospitalized but not in intensive care. Frontline personnel were driven to the point of complete exhaustion due not only to the lack of curative treatments or vaccines, supportive equipment, and protective supplies, but also to the enormous burden of people dying at an incredibly rapid rate with only the caregivers at their sides.

THE RECOGNITION OF HEALTH DISPARITIES

There certainly was no great concern on behalf of national political leaders about the disproportionate toll this virus was taking on the lives of Black, Latinx, and Native American people in this country. Their value was not appreciated.

Data released by the Centers for Disease Control and Prevention showed that through May 2020, Black and Latinx residents in the United States were three times as likely to become infected with COVID-19 and twice as likely to die from it than White residents across all age groups. Consistent with the historical past of our nation, our leadership was failing to respond adequately to this disparity.

As a physician who directed an ambulatory care center serving predominantly Black and Latinx families in the Bronx, I am well-aware of health disparities in these populations. As I described in Chapter 2, to manage some of these disparities, my staff and I went beyond our mission of delivering primary care.

In addition to providing health education programs, food supplement resources, and dental and mental health services, we also participated in a school health consortium. This innovative approach to delivering healthcare to children involved multiple ambulatory care centers that put healthcare providers on-site in schools in 9 of the 10 school districts in the Bronx.

A unique feature to this consortium was a peer education program called "The Health Angels." Fifth graders were educated about basic concepts on good health habits. They then gave presentations to the children in the younger children, who were riveted to the fifth graders' every word. I consider the Health Angels program to be an early example of facilitating leadership development and cultivating emergent leaders. We did not rectify all the disparities, but it was a definitive action to engage everyone to be part of the effort to change the circumstances.

As a medical student in the 1970s, I was taught that the mortality rate for Black infants was three times that of White infants. As an intern and resident, I was deeply disturbed to see some nurses take their time or completely ignore Black adolescent patients suffering the agonizing pain of a sickle cell crisis. When I asked why they were not attentive to these patients, the nurses often responded, "They are probably drug addicts."

As a practicing physician, I was acutely aware of the disproportionate number of hospitalizations of Black and Latinx children for conditions such as asthma and bronchitis. Similarly, their parents and grandparents frequently presented to our clinic with poorly managed diabetes and high blood pressure. The factors that contribute to these circumstances are many, but much can be traced to institutional, cultural, or systemic racism. Unfortunately, this is as true in 2021 as it was several decades ago.

In her article "For Black Women, Being Pregnant Can Be a Matter of Life and Death," S.V. Ramaswamy chronicles the disturbing death rate of pregnant

Black women and how they are treated by some providers. According to the most recent analysis by the Centers for Disease Control and Prevention conducted between 2006 and 2017, Black women die in childbirth at a rate two and a half times that of White women. Social determinants such as income, level of education, or where they lived were not relevant to the outcome. Implicit and explicit bias are primary factors.

Ramaswamy shares stories that range from a nutritionist advising a pregnant Black woman to eat leftover fried chicken as a high protein snack to manage blood sugar to a woman's concerns about being completely ignored. These vignettes, at a minimum, illustrate a lack of empathy, respect, or compassion. At their worst, they represent pure negligence.

To begin to understand the cultural origin of this treatment of Black Americans, one can turn to the book by Harriet A. Washington, *Medical Apartheid*. Washington meticulously documents the history of medical experimentation on Black Americans from colonial years to 2006 and establishes a framework for the belief that Black Americans are inferior and not worthy of respect or dignity. This is discussed in greater detail in the section on social injustice and systemic racism.

THE IMPACT ON THE ECONOMY

The COVID-19 pandemic has ripped through the U.S. economy, affecting large and small businesses, the labor force, and all dependent entities, including individual households. The major exception was the stock market, which had been at high valuation levels before the pandemic struck and, in spite of a few radical fluctuations, remained at near-record highs. Unfortunately, those who are at the greatest risk and suffering the most are not invested in the stock market.

The stock market did not reflect two major competing forces: managing the health crisis and stabilizing the economy. With no clear, comprehensive national directive, some state and local leaders began to formulate their own aggressive plans, especially in New York, New Jersey, and Connecticut, which were among the hardest hit in the first wave of the pandemic. Some leaders maintained that the economy could not be stabilized without first controlling the virus, and thus mandated stay-at-home, social distancing, and mask mandates. Other leaders chose to open businesses without social distancing or mask mandates with the intent to save businesses and the economy, even as infection and death rates rose to unprecedented numbers.

Initially, all non-essential businesses closed. Those who had the financial and technical resources to set up remote operations did so. The impact on the rise in unemployment was immediate. Maintenance, security, and food service staff were no longer needed. Mass transportation use plummeted. The gasoline sales dropped dramatically. Small businesses such as hair salons, barber shops, and fitness centers went out of business. Restaurants, which were subject to severe restrictions, tried everything to comply and survive; yet, many had to close permanently. The unemployment rate rivaled that of the Great Depression.

The loss of income was most significant for those households that could least afford it. Low-income Black and Latinx families with children experienced the greatest economic hardship secondary to COVID-related income loss. They were at significant risk of falling behind in paying bills, meeting rent or mortgage obligations, and having food on the table. All of these circumstances had a domino effect on other areas of the economy.

When rent fees are not paid, landlords find it increasingly difficult to maintain properties and pay taxes. A deficit in tax revenues ultimately impacted the ability to provide essential municipal services. The loss of income may mean that needed medical care or prescription drugs are not obtained in an attempt to have enough money to buy food. Unfortunately, these efforts were not enough, resulting in hundreds of thousands of families standing in lines for free food.

THE FAILURE OF LEADERSHIP

Rather than view the pandemic as a global public health crisis, political leaders in the U.S. politicized the pandemic to the detriment of every citizen of this nation. The pandemic was no longer viewed as a national health crisis that should command everyone's attention and generate a unified focus on how to manage it. The pandemic had become yet another area of contention in a nation deeply divided along political ideologies.

In my view, many of the leadership principles discussed throughout this book have been absent or poorly executed, beginning with the failure to recognize the value of all those who are being led. The leaders' failures were manifested at multiple levels.

The leader who had knowledge of a deadly virus that would impact the lives of millions of Americans deliberately did the following:

- Withheld the information from the public.
- Pretended that it would quickly disappear on its own.
- Ignored or failed to follow the guidance of medical professionals and scientific data.
- Hesitated to take every step, activate every resource at his disposal to provide the available tools and services to contain the spread and care for the sick and dying.
- Failed to demonstrate the behavior or encourage the actions that could save lives.
- Called the scientific experts "idiots" and relied on individuals with no expertise in the relevant scientific field for guidance.

This was clearly the antithesis of a leader who values others. It was the prototype of a narcissistic, autocratic, and self-absorbed individual who is incapable of seeing beyond his own quest for power. This was a leader who did not want to listen or learn. The only counsel he desired was that which agreed with his own. He had no desire to engage, empathize, or support those who were sick and dying or their families who were suffering deep anguish over their inability to be with their loved ones.

Rather than build upon, modify, or utilize work that had been done before, the leader chose to ignore, discard, or undo it. Instead of stepping up to be accountable and responsible for developing a well-coordinated and collaborative approach to meet the needs of the nation, the leader at the highest level chose to deflect that responsibility to others.

Equally disturbing was the dissemination of misinformation or disinformation. This resulted in a fragmented and sometimes chaotic approach to managing the pandemic. People were confused and uncertain of what or who to believe.

An authoritarian, narcissistic leader can be transformational, but unlike the examples I've highlighted in this book, the leader did not lead the nation from where it was to where it needed to be. Instead, the leader's primary objective was to use the nation to get to where he wanted to be. Thankfully, leaders in other areas emerged to move us in the right direction.

THE IMPACT ON EDUCATION

The impact of the pandemic on the educational system at every level, from preschool to college, was monumental. Fortunately, the leaders in many educational systems responded to the crisis with a sense of urgency and focused assessment of scientific data. The higher education leaders who were aware of the severity of the coming pandemic early on did not deny its severity nor try to keep their constituents uninformed or misinformed. Instead, they formed medical advisory panels and discussed potential plans to deal with the COVID pandemic. They convened all essential personnel in their respective institutions to develop a strategy for safely going forward and effectively managing the crisis.

The best leaders informed their leadership teams of the facts as they knew them and sought the input of those who would be responsible for executing the tasks relating to their areas of expertise. With the health and safety of everyone as a primary concern, many educational systems suspended in-person classes and moved completely to remote learning. The shutting down of in-person learning also meant the end of athletic competitions and extracurricular activities. Equally traumatic was the fact that for many students from elementary school through college, there would be no graduation ceremonies or other traditional year-end events.

Converting to remote learning meant that teachers had to be trained to conduct remote learning. It required that every student had a laptop or tablet and internet access. This was not possible in many areas across the country. Some corporations and individuals stepped up to provide free internet access and laptops. School districts not only provided laptops but also prepared free bagged lunches for curbside pickup.

The consequences of remote learning on students were multi-factorial. Students could not look forward to eating lunch with classmates, expending energy during P.E., or chatting with peers. They were deprived of those essential social and emotional interactions. Parents and caregivers experienced enormous stress. They not only had to monitor the progress of the student's work assignments but also had to cope with the periods of frustration, technical challenges, and fatigue that could occur at any moment.

For those parents who had jobs, keeping them was a major challenge. As they progressed through the pandemic, the stress has only intensified as schools had to alternate between in-person and remote learning determined by the number of positive COVID cases in a school system.

A NATION RESPONDED

Leaders at all levels demonstrated genuine compassion, empathy, and a capacity to care about others. America is frequently described as a nation deeply divided by political, social, and racial issues. However, the people's response to helping one another during this pandemic tells another story. Doctors and nurses left their loved ones to travel across the country to places in dire need of their services. They joined the exhausted frontline workers to care for the sickest COVID patients. Some individuals came not knowing where they would sleep, but were willing to commit to working 12-hour shifts for three consecutive weeks.

In March 2020, when New York City hospitals were being inundated with COVID-19 patients, NYU Medical School, in conjunction with all appropriate regulatory and governing agencies, took an unprecedented step to help. The school facilitated the early departure of the graduating class so they could join in the effort to battle the pandemic. Several community organizations and YMCAs offered childcare and other services for healthcare workers. The American Dental Association and state dental associations urged local dentists to donate their personal protective equipment to local hospitals. Multiple resources helped caregivers and their families cope with the emotional and mental health stress related to the pandemic.

Well before the president decided to use the Defense Protection Act to compel manufacturers to produce equipment and protective items to benefit the country, automakers including Ford, GM, Subaru, and Tesla had already seized the initiative to lead change. They began producing ventilators and N95 masks. This effort was duplicated by other smaller companies and individuals all trying to take definitive action to help. Additional companies such as General Electric, Medtronic, Royal Phillips, and 3M joined the efforts after the Defense Protection Act was invoked. The leaders of these organizations saw what was needed and took action.

As the pandemic continued to drain the resources of the American workforce, Congress and the president passed and signed a massive infusion into the economy: the CARES Act. This allowed millions of Americans to survive financially. Yet, millions continue to struggle to feed their families.

Dozens of faith-based organizations and community service organizations have mobilized their resources to help feed those who are food insecure. One transformational leader stands out in this effort.

Chef José Andrés is the founder and leader of the nonprofit organization World Central Kitchen. His visionary leadership has created a global empowerment organization with a mission that focuses on education, health, jobs, and social enterprise, as well as feeding vast numbers of people. Over the past decade, his work in storm-ravaged places like the Bahamas, Haiti, Puerto Rico, and Houston has become legendary. When World Central Kitchen partnered with restaurants to help feed those who were food insecure in the pandemic, the partnership provided more than 30 million meals in over 400 hundred cities in the U.S. This included delivery of meals to senior citizens confined to their homes.

These examples and many more showed a nation of incredibly resilient, compassionate, and innovative people. They demonstrated many principles of the People Value Proposition. They saw the value in others. They exemplified the fact that leadership can occur at any point and is not dependent on one's level in society. Their leadership was validated not by what they said but by what they did.

However, our will to survive was further tested in 2020.

SOCIAL INJUSTICE AND SYSTEMIC RACISM

The death of George Floyd generated a collective outcry for social justice unlike any other in my lifetime. For a moment, my spirits were lifted with the vision of an enlightened America that realized there was still much work to be done to achieve greatness. My vision was not that greatness was an endpoint but rather a continuous process — a process in which everyone is engaged, and everyone is valued. I soon realized that many still have no desire to be engaged in the process. Perhaps because social injustice and systemic racism have existed for so long, it is considered normal by many and not an aberrant state of existence for people of color.

As a Black man who has been fortunate to live beyond my life expectancy, my perspective of injustice and racism extends beyond current events. What I have seen and heard, read about, and experienced shapes my concept of the meaning of "Black Lives Matter." My concept is not a scholarly dissertation, but merely a reflection or expression of the collective images and thoughts seared into my mind.

When I was nine, I saw a photo of the mutilated face of Emit Till, a 14-year-old Black child. He had been beaten to death by White men for allegedly whistling at a White woman. At 19 I read, *100 Years of Lynchings* by Ralph Ginzburg, a grizzly account of some of the 5,000 lynchings of Black individuals in the United States between 1859 and 1959. Apart from the graphic, horrific things done to these people, equally disturbing was the fact that the lynchings were publicized as social events to which families brought their children. I watched the savage beating of Rodney King and the strangulation of Eric Garner, and after the death of George Floyd, I asked,

Why didn't these and other events trigger a collective outcry for justice and an end to racism? Why has it continued with the death of a young Black woman asleep in her bed or the shooting of an unarmed Black man multiple times in the back in front of his children? When did this begin?

The preamble to the Constitution of the United States declares, "We hold these truths to be self-evident, that all men are created equal, that they are endowed by their Creator with certain inalienable rights, among them Life, Liberty and the Pursuit of happiness." These tenets were never meant to include Black men and women. The social injustice and systemic racism people of color have experienced is a perception of "Whiteness" that has been impregnated into the minds of those who have passed it from generation to generation, century to century. Further evidence of this can be seen in the initial experience of Italian immigrants who came to America in the 19th century.

In his *New York Times* article "How Italians Became White," Brent Staples writes that dark-skinned Italians were described, in the press, as members of a criminal race, "kinky-haired," "dago," and "guinea" — terms usually applied to enslaved Africans. The author also describes how 11 Italian immigrant men accused of killing a police chief were lynched. That same mentality that triggers a perception of who you are based solely on the color of your skin persists to this day.

It is the reason that Black parents across America have a conversation with their sons and daughters about how to act when they give them the keys to the car. It was the reason I was almost brought to tears when I heard that my six-year-old grandson, who was aware of George Floyd's death, was now afraid to be seen by the police.

As a physician, my perception of Black Lives Matter goes beyond police brutality and lynchings. Just as bad police officers need to be weeded out, the same is true of the bad doctors and lawyers. Physician leaders have a specific responsibility to help identify and report physicians engaged in the inappropriate prescribing of opioids, subjecting patients to unnecessary tests, procedures, and treatments. Physician leaders must also ensure the integrity of electronic health records generated in their offices or organizations.

I am equally concerned about the Black lives lost to gun violence perpetrated by Black and Latino gangs and other individuals who believe the only resolution to any issue is the use of violence. In an urban community close to my home, 21 individuals had been killed by violent gangs or individuals in the first 10 months of 2020, more than had occurred by the hands of police in the past decade. As a pediatrician, I'm deeply troubled about the children lost to child abuse, drug and alcohol abuse.

There is no panacea for all that is wrong, but we can do better.

When I consider the progression of Black people in this country from slavery to segregation, Jim Crow, and the continued efforts to suppress our vote, limit economic advancement and determine where you live, a caste system seems to be an accurate depiction of what constitutes social injustice and systemic racism. Native Americans, Asians, and immigrant populations coming across our southern border have experienced similar injustices.

My awareness of social injustice and systemic racism, experience with good and bad leaders, and full acceptance of the People Value Proposition compelled me to accept a leadership role that could begin to make a difference.

In Spring 2020, the president of the Board of Trustees at Marist College asked me to serve as the chairman of the Diversity and Inclusion Committee. To develop a meaningful action agenda for the college, I conducted listening sessions to learn and try to understand what every diverse group (Black, Latino, Asian, White, LGBTQ, etc.) was experiencing. I also wanted these groups to represent every segment of the college community (students, faculty, staff, administration, and alumni). I was disturbed by what I heard, especially because I had chaired the Student Life Committee for nearly 10 years. During that time, I never heard any of the discordant diversity and inclusion issues revealed in the listening sessions. A number of common themes were evident:

- Respect me for who I am
- Strive to understand my perspective through mandatory training and an enriched curriculum on social injustice, equality, and systemic racism.
- Don't make assumptions about what I think, want, or need.
- Don't exclude me, but allow me to have my own space.
- Give me an equal opportunity to participate and compete.
- Support me when I need it.

I recognize that the way forward is to provide an educational experience that enables members of the college community to begin to reframe everyone's thinking using some of the tools and concepts relating to diversity, inclusion, and bias described in this book. The students must graduate with a greater insight into the complexities of diversity, equity, and inclusion. They must also have the confidence, consciousness, and commitment that they can make a difference.

Similarly, those who teach must serve as the vanguard for the development of new leaders of change. The year 2020 is often referred to as the year from hell, given the many challenges it presented. However, it can also be viewed as a year that drew upon the inner strengths of a nation, a year in which individuals from every walk of life demonstrated an enormous capacity to empathize, care, and support one another.

It was a year that encouraged more people than ever to acknowledge the need to listen to each other, learn from each other, and live with each other. They are the new leaders of a necessary cultural transformation. There is a new awareness that social injustice and systemic racism are real, that there are things we can do to mitigate the ravages of disease and slow the progression of climate change.

To overcome the challenges before us, each of us must open our minds to **SEE** what needs to be done, incorporate these actions into our lives and **DO** what must be done; and **TEACH** others by your example, not just your words. We must live the **People Value Proposition**.

REFERENCES

Baldwin R. Automakers Step Up to Challenge of Helping in Coronavirus Pandemic. *Car and Driver*. March 24, 2020. www.caranddriver.com/news/a31916026/trump-defense-production-act-automakers/

Bauer L, Broady K, Edelberg W, and O'Donnell J. Ten Facts About COVID-19 and the U.S. Economy. The Brookings Institute. September 17, 2020. www.brookings.edu/research/ten-facts-about-covid-19-and-the-u-s-economy.

Burton M. The Story Behind the José Andrés Nonprofit Serving Hurricane Dorian Victims. Eater. September 5, 2019. www.eater.com/2017/11/10/16623204/world-central-kitchen-jose-andres-bahamas-puerto-rico-haiti-houston

ChefsforAmerica—World Central Kitchen. https//wck.org/chefsforamerica

Jayawickrama S. Developing Managers and Leaders: Experiences and Lessons from International NGOs. Hauser Center-Harvard Humanitarian Initiative Special Report, John F. Kennedy School of Government, Harvard University; 2011.

Kosoff M. Amazon Has a White Man Problem: Beyond Social Justice, Experts Call It a Business Liability. OneZero. February 27, 2019.

McAfee M, Pedersen C, Kim D, et al. Doctors, Nurses From Across the US Step Up To Help NYC on the Coronavirus Front Lines. ABC News. April 9, 2020. https://abcnews.go.com/US/doctors-nurses-us-step-nyc-coronavirus-front-lines/story?id=70049109

Oppel Jr RA, Gebeloff R, Lai KK, et.al. The Fullest Look Yet at the Racial Inequity of Coronavirus. *The New York Times*. July 5, 2020. www.nytimes.com/interactive/2020/07/05/us/coronavirus-latinos-african-americans-cdc-data.html

Ginzburg R. *100 Years of Lynchings*. Baltimore: Black Classic Press; 1962.

Patton M. The Impact of COVID-19 on U.S. Economy and Financial Markets. *Forbes*. October 12, 2020. https://www.forbes.com/sites/mikepatton/2020/10/12/the-impact-of-covid-19-on-us-economy-and-financial-markets/?sh=7fbb5f8d2d20 Ramaswamy SV. Black Women Are Dying in Childbirth More Often Than White Women. Loloud. com September 8, 2020. https://www.lohud.com/in-depth/news/2020/09/08/as-black-woman-when-youre-pregnant-your-own-advocate/5442487002/

Staples B. How Italians Became White. *The New York Times*. October 12, 2019. https://www.nytimes.com/interactive/2019/10/12/opinion/columbus

Washington HA. *Medical Apartheid: The Dark History of Medical Experimentation on Black Americans from Colonial Times to the Present*. New York: Harlem Moon 2006.

Wilkerson I. Caste: The Origins of Our Discontents. New York: Random House; 2020.

RESOURCES

Abrashoff DM. *It's Your Ship: Management Techniques from the Best Damn Ship in the Navy*. New York: Grand Central Publishing 2012.

Acho E. *Uncomfortable Conversations with a Black Man*. New York: Flatiron Books; 2020.

Adkins A. Majority of U.S. Employees Not Engaged Despite Gains in 2014. Gallup. January 28, 2015. https://news.gallup.com/poll/181289/majority-employees-not-engaged-despite-gains-2014.aspx.

Alliance for Board Diversity. *Missing Pieces: The 2018 Board Diversity Census of Women and Minorities on Fortune 500 Boards*. ABD and Deloitte. 2019. www.catalyst.org/research/missing-pieces-report-the-2018-board-diversity-census-of-women-and-minorities-on-fortune-500-boards.

Angood P. *All Physicians Are Leaders: Reflections on Inspiring Change Together for Better Healthcare*. Washington, D.C. American Association for Physician Leadership; 2020.

Anthony SD and Schwartz EI. What the Best Transformational Leaders Do. *Harvard Business Review*. 2017. https://hbr.org/2017/05what-the-best-transformational-leaders-do

Baldwin R. Automakers Step Up to Challenge of Helping in Coronavirus Pandemic. *Car and Driver*. March 24, 2020. www.caranddriver.com/news/a31916026/trump-defense-production-act-automakers.

Bass BM. *Leadership and Performance Beyond Expectations*. New York: Free Press; 1985.

Bauer L, Broady K, Edelberg W, and O'Donnell J. Ten Facts About COVID-19 and the U.S. Economy. The Brookings Institute. September 17, 2020. www.brookings.edu/research/ten-facts-about-covid-19-and-the-u-s-economy.

Bossidy L and Charan R. *Execution: The Discipline of Getting Things Done*. New York: Crown Business; 2022.

Boulton C. What Is Digital Transformation? A Necessary Disruption. CIO. June 24, 2021. https://www.cio.com/article/230425/what-is-digital-transformation-a-necessary-disruption.html.

Burton M. The Story Behind the José Andrés Nonprofit Serving Hurricane Dorian Victims. Eater. September 5, 2019. www.eater.com/2017/11/10/16623204/world-central-kitchen-jose-andres-bahamas-puerto-rico-haiti-houston

Burton V. Successful Women Think Differently: 9 Habits to Make You Happier. Healthier & More Resilient. Eugene, Oregon: Harvest House; 2012.

Cain S. *Quiet: The Power of Introvert in a World That Can't Stop Talking.* New York: Random House; 2013.

Canwell A and Stockton H. (2019). Leaders at All Levels: Close the Gap Between Hype and Readiness. Deloitte Insights. 2019. www2.deloitte.com/us/en/insights/authers/adam-canwell/heather-stockton.htm.

Caraher L. Millennials & Management: The Essential Guide to Making It Work at Work. New York: Routledge; 2014.

Chapman B and Sisodia R. *Everybody Matters: The Extraordinary Power of Caring for Your People like Family.* New York: Penguin Random House; 2015.

ChefsforAmerica—World Central Kitchen. https://wck.org/chefsforamerica

Chin JL. Diversity Leadership: Influences of Ethnicity, Gender and Minority Status. *Open Journal of Leadership.* 2013; 2(1):1-10.

Cockrell L. *Creating Magic: 10 Common Leadership Strategies from a Life at Disney.* New York: Doubleday; 2008.

Cohen WA. *Drucker on Leadership: New Lessons from the Father of Modern Management.* San Francisco: Jossey-Bass; 2010.

Collins J. *Good to Great: Why Some Companies Make the Leap . . . and Others Don't.* New York: Harper Collins 2001.

Colmen D. 12 Choices That Lead to Your Success. Dallas, TX: Cornerstone Leadership Institute; 2005.

Corporate Leadership Council. Building the High-Performance Workplace: A Quantitative Analysis of the Effectiveness of Performance Management Strategies. 2002. www.corporateleadershipcouncil.com.

Cuddy A. *Presence: Bringing Your Boldest Self to Your Biggest Challenges.* New York: Little Brown and Company; 2015.

Cummings S, Bridgeman T, and Brown KG. (Sept. 2015). Unfreezing Change as Three Steps: Rethinking Kurt Lewin's Legacy for Change Management. *Human Relations*. 2016; 69(1).

Dame J and Gedmin, J. Six Principles for Developing Humility as a Leader. *Harvard Business Review*. October 9, 2013.

Druskat VU, Sala F, and Mount G. *Linking Emotional Intelligence and Performance at Work: Current Research Evidence with Individuals and Groups*. Mahwah, New Jersey: Lawrence Erlbaum Associates; 2006.

Dubey R and Hirsch AS. Viewpoint: Building a Business Case for Diversity and Inclusion. SHRM. March 19, 2018. www.shrm.org/resourcesandtools/ hr-topics/behavioral-competencies/global-and-cultural-effectiveness/pages/ viewpoint-building-a-business-case-for-diversity-and-inclusion.aspx

Edubilla.com. George de Mestral—Famous Inventor. www.edubilla.com/ inventor/george-de-mestral.

Ehman J. Religious Diversity: Practical Points for Health Care Providers. Penn Medicine. April 2007. www.uphs.upenn.edu/pastoral/resed/diversity_ points.html

Epstein D. Range: *Why Generalists Triumph in a Specialized World*. New York: Riverhead Books; 2019.

Eswaran V. The Business Case for Diversity in the Workplace Is Now Overwhelming. World Economic Forum. April 29, 2019. www.weforum.org/ agenda/2019/04/business-case-for-diversity-in-the-workplace.

Foster WZ. *The Negro People in American History*. New York: International Publishers; 1954.

Frankl VE. Man's Search for Meaning. Boston, Mass: Beacon Press; 2006.

Gallup. (2014). Majority of American Workers Not Engaged Despite Gains. Gallup. 2014. *wwwgallup.com/poll/181289/majority-aspx*

Gallup. How Millennials Want to Work and Live. Gallup. 2016. https:// enviableworkplace.com/wp-content/uploads/Gallup-How-Millennials-Want-To-Work.pdf.

Ginzburg R. *100 Years of Lynchings*. Baltimore: Black Classic Press; 1962.

Gladwell M. *Outliers: The Story of Success*. New York: Little Brown and Company; 2008.

Gladwell M. *Talking to Strangers: What We Should Know About the People We Don't Know.* New York: Little Brown and Company; 2019.

Goleman D. *Emotional Intelligence: Why It Can Matter More Than IQ.* New York: Bantam; 1995.

Goler L, Gale J, Harrington B, and Grant A. Why People Really Quit Their Jobs. *Harvard Business Review.* July 11, 2018. https://hbr.org/2018/01/why-people-really-quit-their-jobs

Goodwin J. Amazon Adds More Executive Diversity with the Appointment of First Black Woman to Its Senior Leadership Team. CNN Business. August 25, 2020. www.cnn.com/2020/08/25/tech/amazon-first-black-executive-senior-leadership-team-bezos/index.html

Gorman CK. *The Silent Language of Leaders: How Body Language Can Help or Hurt How You Lead.* San Francisco: Jossey-Bass; 2011.

Harvard Business Review. *Best of HBR on Emotionally Intelligent Leadership, 2nd Edition.* Boston: Harvard Business School Publishing Corporation; 2008.

Hasson G. *Mindfulness: Be Mindful. Live in the Moment.* New York: Fall River Press; 2013.

Her Majesty the Queen. www.royal.uk/her-majesty-the-queen

Hobbs J. *The Short and Tragic Life of Robert Peace.* New York: Scribner; 2014.

Horowitz JM, Igielnik R, and Parker K. *Women and Leadership 2018.* Pew Research Center. September 2018. www.pewresearch.org/social-trends/2018/09/20/women-and-leadership-2018/

Hougaard R. The Real Crisis in Leadership. *Forbes.* September 9, 2018.

Hughes M, Patterson LB, and Terrell JB. *Emotional Intelligence in Action: Training and Coaching Activities for Leaders and Managers.* San Francisco: Pfeiffer; 2005.

Hunt V, Prince S, and Dixon-Fyle S. *Delivering through Diversity.* London: McKinsey & Company; 2018.

Hunt V, Prince S, Dixon-Fyle S and Dolan K. *Diversity Wins: How Inclusion Matters.* London: McKinsey & Company; 2020.

Hussain ST, Lei S, et. al. Kurt Lewin's Change Model: A Critical Review of the Role of Leadership and Employee Involvement in Organizational Change. *Journal of Innovation and Knowledge.* 2016; 3: 123-127.

Iacoboni M. *Mirroring People: The Science of Empathy and How We Connect with Others.* New York: Picador; 2008.

Jarrett E. Diversity Is More Than Just the Kind You Can See. TLNT blog. September 20, 2018. www.tlnt.com/the-many-types-of-diversity-should-be-on-your-teams/#:~:text=Diversity%20of%20opinion%2C%20outlook%20and,hire%20people%20similar%20to%20themselves.

Jayawickrama S. Developing Managers and Leaders: Experiences and Lessons from International NGOs. Hauser Center-Harvard Humanitarian Initiative Special Report, John F. Kennedy School of Government; 2011.

Juckett G. Caring for Latino Patients. *American Family Physician.* 2013; 87(1):48-54.

Kark R, Shamir B, and Chen G. The Two Faces of Transformational Leadership: Empowerment and Dependency. *Journal of Applied Psychology.* 2003; 88(2):246-255

Kellerman B. *Hard Times: Leadership in America.* Stanford, CA. Stanford University Press; 2014.

Kerns Goodwin D. *Leadership in Turbulent Times.* New York: Simon and Schuster; 2018.

Kerpen D. *The Art of People: 11 Simple People Skills That Will Get You Everything You Want.* New York: Crown Business; 2016.

Kiel F. *Return on Character: The Real Reason Leaders and Their Companies Win.* Boston: Harvard Business Review Press; 2015.

Kosoff M. Amazon Has a White Man Problem: Beyond Social Justice, Experts Call It a Business Liability. OneZero. February 27, 2019. https://onezero.medium.com/amazon-has-a-white-man-problem-179e9759f35b

Kotter J and Rathgeber H. *Our Iceberg Is Melting: Changing and Succeeding Under Any Conditions.* Chicago: Macmillan; 2005.

Kumagai AK and Lypson ML. Beyond Cultural Competence: Critical Consciousness, Social Justice, and Multicultural Education. *Academic Medicine.* 2009. 84(6):782-787

Ladd K. 120 Women Who Changed Our World. *Good Housekeeping.* March 2, 2108. https://www.goodhousekeeping.com/life/inspirational-stories/g2239/women-who-changed-our-world/?slide=14

Malala Yousafzai. Britannica. www.britannica.com/biography/Malala-Yousafzai

Manolio TA, Bult CJ, et. al. Genomic Medicine Year in Review: *The American Journal of Human Genetics.* 2019;105:1072-1075.

Marston C. *Motivating The "What's in It for Me?" Workforce: Manage Across the Generational Divide and Increase Profits.* Hoboken, NJ: John Wiley & Sons; 2007.

McAfee M, Pedersen C, Kim D, et al. Doctors, Nurses From Across the US Step Up To Help NYC on the Coronavirus Front Lines. ABC News. April 9, 2020. https://abcnews.go.com/US/doctors-nurses-us-step-nyc-coronavirus-front-lines/story?id=70049109

McKay M and Fanning P. *Self-Esteem.* Oakland, CA: New Harbinger Publications; 2000.

Miles R. *Leading* Corporate *Transformation: A Blueprint for Renewal.* San Francisco: Jossey-Bass Publishers; 1997.

Miller P. My 4 Principles of Digital Leadership. LinkedIn. 2016. www.linkedin.com/pulse/my-4principles-digital-leadership-p

Moldoveanu M and Narayandas D. The Future of Leadership Development. *Harvard Business Review.* March-April 2019. https://hbr.org/2019/03/the-future-of-leadership-development

Murphy SA. *Leading a Multigenerational Workforce.* Washington, DC: AARP; 2007.

National Institutes of Health, National Human Genome Research Institute. *www.genome.gov/dna-day/15waysGenomicsInfluencesOurWorld*

Noland M and Moran T. Study: Firms with More Women in the C-Suite Are More Profitable. *Harvard Business Review.* February 2016. https://hbr.org/2016/02/study-firms-with-more-women-in-the-c-suite-are-more-profitable

Oppel Jr RA, Gebeloff R, Lai KK, et. al. The Fullest Look Yet at the Racial Inequity of Coronavirus. *The New York Times.* July 5, 2020. www.nytimes.

com/interactive/2020/07/05/us/coronavirus-latinos-african-americans-cdc-data.html https://www.nytimes.com/interactive/2020/07/05//us/coronavirus-lati

Patton M. The Impact of COVID-19 on U.S. Economy and Financial Markets. *Forbes*. October 12, 2020. https://www.forbes.com/sites/mikepatton/2020/10/12/the-impact-of-covid-19-on-us-economy-and-financial-markets/?sh=7fbb5f8d2d20

Ramaswamy SV. Black Women Are Dying in Childbirth More Often Than White Women. Loloud.com September 8, 2020. https://www.lohud.com/in-depth/news/2020/09/08/as-black-woman-when-youre-pregnant-your-own-advocate/5442487002/

Phillips KW. How Diversity Makes Us Smarter. *Scientific American*. October 2104. https://www.scientificamerican.com/article/how-diversity-makes-us-smarter.

Pinkett R, Robinson J, and Patterson P. *Black Faces in White Places: 10 Game-Changing Strategies to Achieve Success and Find Greatness*. New York: AMACOM; 2011.

Prasad V. Stop the Medical School "Arms Race." *Medscape Oncology*. January 31, 2020.

Ristino R. *The Agile Manager's Guide to Managing Change*. Bristol, VT.: Velocity Business Publishing; 2000.

Roberts W. *Leadership Secrets of Atilla the Hun*. New York: Warner Books; 1985.

Rosen B. Leadership Journeys — Mary Barra: Harnessing Kinetic Energy at General Motors. IEDP Viewpoint. January 2014. www.iedp.com/articles/leadership-journeys-mary-barra.

Rothberg H. *The Perfect Mix: Everything I Learned About Leadership I Learned as a Bartender*. New York: Simon and Schuster; 2017.

Sanborn M. *You Don't Need a Title to be a Leader: How Anyone, Anywhere Can Make a Positive Difference*. New York: Doubleday; 2006.

Scroggins C. *How to Lead When You're Not in Charge: Leveraging Influence When You Lack Authority*: Grand Rapids, MI: Zondervan-Harper Collins; 2017.

Secretan L. *Inspirational Leadership: Destiny, Calling and Cause*. Canada: Macmillan; 1999.

SHRM. Fair Labor Standards Act of 1938. SHRM HR Public Policy Issues. www.shrm.org/hr-today/public-policy/hr-public-policy-issues/pages/fairlaborstandardsactof1938.aspx

Sinek S. *Start With Why: How Great Leaders Inspire Everyone to Take Action*. New York: Penguin Group; 2009.

Sisodia R, Wolfe D, and Sheth J. *Firms of Endearment: How World Class Companies Profit from Passion and Purpose*. Upper Saddle River, N.J.: Pearson Education; 2014.

Stacy S. *50 Nonclinical Careers for Physicians: Fulfilling, Meaningful and Lucrative Alternatives to Direct Patient Care*. Washington, D.C. American Association for Physician Leadership 2020.

Staples B. How Italians Became White. *The New York Times*. October 12, 2019. https://www.nytimes.com/interactive/2019/10/12/opinion/columbus

Strecher VJ. *Life on Purpose: How Living for What Matters Most Changes Everything*. New York: Harper Collins; 2016.

Swartz J and Peister B. Human Capital Trends 2014. Deloitte Insights. 2014. https://www2.deloitte.com/us/en/insights/focus/human-capital-trends/2014/human-capital-trends-2014-survey-top-10-findings.html

Tervalon M and Murray-Garcia J. Cultural Humility Verses Cultural Competence: A Critical Distinction In Defining Training Outcomes In Multicultural Education. *Journal of Health Care for the Poor and Underserved*. 1998;9: 117-125.

The White House. First Lady Michelle Obama. https://obamawhitehouse.archives.gov/administration/first-lady-michelle-obama

Thompson K, and Mac Austin H. *The Face of Our Past*. Bloomington, IN: Indiana University Press; 1999.

Towers Watson. 2014 Global Workforce Study. 2015.

U.S. Bureau of Labor Statistics. Highlights of Women's Earnings in 2018. BLS Reports. November 2019. www.bls.gov/opub/reports/womens-earnings/2018/home.htm

Walker S. *The Captain Class: The Hidden Force that Creates the World's Greatest Teams.* New York: Random House; 2017.

Walters JD. *The Art of Leadership.* New York: MJF Books; 1987.

Washington HA. *Medical Apartheid: The Dark History of Medical Experimentation on Black Americans from Colonial Times to the Present.* New York: Harlem Moon 2006.

Welch J. *Jack: Straight from the Gut.* New York: Warner Books; 2001.

Wilkerson I. Caste: The Origins of Our Discontents. New York: Random House; 2020.

Zweig D. Managing the "Invisibles." *Harvard Business Review.* May 2014. https://hbr.org/2014/05/managing-the-invisibles